The New Model of Selling

Praise for *The New Model of Selling*

Thinking from the prospect's perspective is one thing, but presenting a tactical and replicable way to create a clear sales structure that can win success in any industry, is another perspective completely.

What *The New Model of Selling* does so well is takes good ideas that make selling 'human,' and gives them a tactical framework that is easy to follow and execute on. It's a work of simple sales genius with a methodology that's so aligned with how humans are naturally wired, that the process is seamless from connection to close.

— **Ryan Serhant**, Founder and CEO of SERHANT and
New York Times Best-selling Author

No matter who your customer is, the industry you serve, whether B2B, B2C or if its just plain persuading people in your everyday life – *The New Model of Selling* demystifies and simplifies influence and persuasion giving anyone dealing with humans day to day, a word-class way to communicate.

— **Brendan Kane**, Managing Director of Hook Point and
Author of *One Million Followers* and *Hook Point*

For all those in-person, by-phone or online salespeople who become wracked with self-doubt since customers stopped behaving or buying like they used to...*The New Model of Selling* explains WHY this is so! It also shows you how to fix it fast, and become wildly successful at your craft. This book approaches sales from an all-new, different direction and serves as a 'RED PILL' that will open your eyes to a whole new world of possibility and unlimited earning potential.

— **Russell Brunson**, Founder of Clickfunnels

The New Model of Selling by Acuff and Miner is a must-read for anyone in the business of persuading others. Far too many people in the business of influence have not been taught how to use what we know about human behavior to be truly persuasive. This book will give the reader ideas on how to dramatically reduce sales resistance and how to be far more effective in any persuasion situation.

— **Buzz Williams**, Head Basketball Coach, Texas A & M

The New Model of Selling is a book only for people in sales who truly aspire to be seen by their customers and prospects as the consummate professional that is unlike the vast majority of people they have encountered in sales.

— **Shae Maughmer**, Vice President and General Manager,
Lundbeck Pharmaceuticals

Jerry's deep experience base and his unequaled ability to translate and teach selling skills, has changed my life, and I'm confident he can change yours. Here, in *The New Model of Selling*, you get two of the worlds' best sales experts guiding you on how to achieve genuine personal impact with your customers in our often bewildering digital and algorithmic world.

— **David Snow**, Senior Vice President, Regeneron Pharmaceuticals

Coaches must be able to persuade, or they can't effectively recruit. *The New Model of Selling* is a terrific resource to help anyone wanting to be exceptional at communicating their value proposition in a no pressure, professional manner in order to succeed far more often than before.

— **Herb Sendek**, Head Basketball Coach, Santa Clara University

Salespeople in any industry will find *The New Model of Selling*, (co-authored by two of the top sales experts in the world) to be a long overdue resource that will wipe out sales resistance and lead to far greater sales results than ever. Furthermore, the practical knowledge outlined in this book can be used by anyone in any business setting. The way it is broken down allows the reader to change some behaviors without sacrificing their own style.

— **Kelly Sullivan**, Senior Vice President of Blue Stream Fiber

In a digital first world, consumers are just different. Analog sales methods are rendered obsolete and ineffective. *The New Model of Selling* holds the keys to success for meeting today's clients when, where, and how they want to be met. Leveraging neuroscience in our sales process has been transformational for us, and it will be for you too.

— **Casey Watkins**, Co-Founder and CEO of
Quility Insurance and Symmetry Financial Group

The New Model of Selling is necessary reading for anyone who sells anything. If you're a salesperson, entrepreneur or manage a team of salespeople, this book shows how to uncover nuggets of information about your prospect's situation and problems that they didn't even know were there! In so doing it pioneers a new process of self-persuasion. Easy to learn and enjoyable to use. If you want better results, make this book your guide to greater sales success.

— **Gerhard Gschwandtner**, CEO of Selling Power Magazine

The
NEW
MODEL
of SELLING

Selling to an
**UNSELLABLE
GENERATION**

JERRY ACUFF
JEREMY MINER

NEW YORK

LONDON • NASHVILLE • MELBOURNE • VANCOUVER

The New Model of Selling

Selling to an Unsellable Generation

Published in New York, New York, by Morgan James Publishing. Morgan James is a trademark of Morgan James, LLC. www.MorganJamesPublishing.com

Proudly distributed by Ingram Publisher Services.

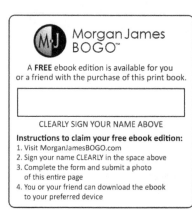

A **FREE** ebook edition is available for you
or a friend with the purchase of this print book.

CLEARLY SIGN YOUR NAME ABOVE

Instructions to claim your free ebook edition:
1. Visit MorganJamesBOGO.com
2. Sign your name CLEARLY in the space above
3. Complete the form and submit a photo
   of this entire page
4. You or your friend can download the ebook
   to your preferred device

ISBN 9781636980119 paperback
ISBN 9781636980126 ebook
Library of Congress Control Number:
2022941673

Cover & Interior Design by:
Christopher Kirk
www.GFSstudio.com

with...

Morgan James is a proud partner of Habitat for Humanity Peninsula
and Greater Williamsburg. Partners in building since 2006.

Get involved today! Visit: www.morgan-james-publishing.com/giving-back

This book is dedicated to the countless sales professionals and sales leaders who have had no choice but to learn, adopt and apply traditional selling techniques conceived in the dinosaur ages of selling.

This disservice has kept incomes stuck, spirits weary and the craft of selling reduced to little more than a rejection-rich numbers game in which only the strongest survive, and fewer still succeed.

Table of Contents

Introduction

Just because something works doesn't mean that it cannot be improved.
—Shuri, *Black Panther*

Those of us in sales these days often find ourselves in an alternative universe that's not so marvelous. Think about it: our old-school, cold-called customer base was killed off years ago by the very technology that we rely on today for survival. The only thing technology hasn't replaced yet, thank goodness, is toilet paper, which still, today, remains an easy sale. We salespeople cannot be wiped away, however, and, while we are armed with the very tools that built the very first car, we find ourselves gazing out into a world of self-driving Teslas, trying to figure out how to keep up.

Shuri, the Princess of Wakanda, the mythical Marvel kingdom's tech guru, wasn't kidding, and she wasn't dubbed by some superhero goobers as the smartest character in the Marvel Cinematic Universe for nothing either. But, at the end of the day, especially in this day and age, not everyone's as fortunate and fictional as Shuri, and they don't have a killer cocktail of genius and vibranium to assist them in their ascents to the throne of whatever kingdom they may be trying to conquer. For those of us in the sales biz, it can often feel like we're the black-and-white Mighty Mouse fighting against an 8K RED Camera to Cloud Technicolor titan such as Captain America.

The world has morphed into something that seems only sustainable in a Marvel universe with us salespeople left channeling our inner superhero, fighting to sell to an unsellable generation that relies on the mighty morphing inter-webs like Spidey weaving his way through a dark and brooding metropolis for, well, everything.

Today's buyers are skeptical and don't trust us—or anyone—like they used to. Because they are armed with excessive amounts of information accessible instantly, they are more distrustful of so-called experts. In fact, some of them may even consider themselves graduates of Google U. and consider themselves experts as well. Who knows, maybe they are, maybe they aren't, but to paraphrase the Notorious B.I.G., mo' Google, mo' problems. Like that pesky paywall you refuse to break with a paid subscription, the barrier is up before you've even uttered a word.

So much of what's been taught about sales isn't just the "OK, Boomer" of our biz—an out-of-touch technique still trying to figure out how to program the VCR—but it's also an impenetrable firewall between us and our clients. These old-school methods may be charming in the same way a black-and-white picture is, but they act as a repellent to positive results. They are meme material—the "How It Began" to the "How It's Going," the old war stories told on repeat by the sales vets of yore. Not that there's anything wrong with that unless, of course, your goal is to make the sale, rather than throw back a few in between bars of a Billy Joel anthem and then go home empty-handed.

Look, nostalgia and history are great, but they're not good enough to be used as ammo on the front lines of today's sales landscape. This is not our daddy's sales force, and it most certainly isn't our grandparents' either. Taking a page from *Star Trek*, it's our mission as salespeople to go beyond what was once thought of as the final frontier "to explore strange new worlds. To seek out new life and new civilizations. To boldly go where no man has gone before!"

Those seeking serious success in sales must navigate the new terrain with fresh ideas, approaches, and techniques. Make like an exasperated Karen after the manager refused to see her and cancel nearly everything you've been taught about sales thus far; using outdated sales methods right now will likely get you canceled in the biz as well.

Yes, yes, you've probably done OK with the outmoded methods. You've managed, but that's just it: you've just managed. You haven't mastered it because you can't watch a TikTok video on a Sony Walkman and it's driving you nuts. No matter how hard you try to play that video with all the techniques you've learned in your career thus far, they just won't play well today, if at all. And you need to see what all the fuss is about. But par for the on-demand generation, you need to see it fast.

We don't believe in wasting time. There are plenty of ways to do that (see: the aforementioned TikTok). This book is the antithesis of a time waster, freeing up your valuable hours and minutes to set yourself apart from other business and sales professionals. But here's the rub: we don't just want to transform your numbers, but also the way you and the world view sales.

This trippy transformation will take "thinking like a customer" to an entirely new level—a human level. No robots, no machines, no Siri, no Alexa; just you and the customer (unless their names happen to be Siri and Alexa, of course). If you're going to become a stellar salesperson, you must define selling in the right way and implement advanced skills that align with human behavior. This is absolutely crucial.

As the Icelandic pop pixie Bjork so sagely sings in her song aptly titled "Human Behavior," To paraphrase the Icelandic pop pixie Bjork, engaging with people is ever so satisfying. It's not just satisfying, it's our MO, the cornerstone of what we believe and how both of us have achieved extraordinary results for decades. Because here's the secret: there is no "unsellable generation"; there's only an incompatible generation. It is your job to adapt to it the way we did.

What we are going to show you will work for any product or service no matter the industry. Whether you are a business owner, sales professional, coach, sales manager, politician, sales executive or leader, this book will assist you and your team with moving more people. As a result, you will have more sales and an easier time procuring them.

The New Model of Selling: Selling to an Unsellable Generation is not just another book with a bunch of great sales tips you'll read and forget about next month. This book is about reframing how you define sales and discovering how to help the customer think for themselves. Revolutionary, right? The New Model of Selling leaves customers with a great experience because you are helping them find and solve their problems. It helps take you from neurotic salesperson to neuro-emotional persuasive rockstar!

Customers feel that you are doing them a favor, and they are paying you money for that. Before, in their eyes, you were likely the stereotypical sleazy salesperson, the green-eyed monster out for a pretty penny. With our model, you are an expert, a trusted authority, a friend, an adviser, and someone they reach out to and share funny memes with. Well, maybe not the latter, but wouldn't it be nice to have the customers gravitate toward you for a change?

This book is not for everybody. This book is not for the person who wants to pound, grind, and grunt to make a sale. How exhausting is that? It is not for the person who wants to stay in the status quo, hoping and praying that somehow they will sell more by doing the same thing. It is not for the person in love with their ego, thinking they know everything about sales and are afraid to adapt to sell more.

This book is for the person who wants to stop chasing sales and get their prospects to start chasing them for a change. It is for those who want to exceed mediocre results by discovering better ideas proven to work! Great salespeople have a growth mindset and are always looking for new ideas to propel them to extraordinary success.

Sure, you can make a decent living selling the old way, pounding the pavement and working hard, but why not learn advanced skills, start working less, but make way more money? Why not follow the path of two sales legends to get where you want to be? Why put yourself through the frustration of playing the numbers game only to continue achieving subpar results? It's all about working smarter and not harder—about doing the fundamental work of reconfiguring everything you thought you knew.

Since you've picked up this book, it's evident you want to get better at your craft because you are dedicated to excellence. Sales is a treacherous plane, but sometimes, the thing holding you back the most is your own thought process because you don't know what you don't know and, frankly, the skills you have been taught just don't work well these days.

By the time you've reached the last chapter, you're going to have a far better understanding of why outdated methods aren't as effective as they once were, have the tools to improve your skills, and be able to maximize your income. You do this not by being persuasive in your own right but by getting the prospect to persuade themselves.

That's right. *This book will show you how to interact with your potential prospects in a way that enables them to persuade themselves.*

In neuroscience sales ninja Weldon Long's book *The Power of Consistency*, he writes, "You can't get new results with old habits. You can't get new results with the same actions you have. You have to do something different."

Let us show you exactly what to do differently, and you are certain to meet unimaginable success! The single most effective way to sell anything to anyone in 2022 is to be a problem finder and a problem solver and not a product pusher.

As Ramonda said in *Black Panther*, "Your father taught you all that warrior nonsense—but he also taught you how to think." Throw in our next-level, cerebral approach to sales and you'll emerge a sales warrior, crushing it in a way only an A-list superhero can.

Who Are We?

Jerry Acuff

I'm Jerry Acuff, CEO of Delta Point, Inc., an Arizona-based company that transforms underperforming sales teams into sales titans, and I have been consulting and speaking extensively on sales and marketing excellence issues for over thirty years. Named one of the top ten sales experts by Global Gurus for six consecutive years, my goal is to uplift others and give my clients the selling secrets I had to discover independently. I know what it is like to be a frustrated person starting in sales. I know what it's like to be working under the old method. Most people don't know this, but I got fired from my first two sales jobs because I couldn't sell. Not one, but two! My second sales position was with Lipton Tea. I had such sales reluctance that I would literally sit in my car for thirty to forty-five minutes to get the courage to meet face-to-face with a customer.

The anxiety was brutal. I concluded that selling was not for me. I then went into teaching and coaching in hopes of becoming a college football coach. I even tried to be a graduate assistant at a college where my high school coach was the head coach. That didn't work out either! I only took a job in sales after getting rejected from graduate school because I was not a very good student in college.

My 2.18 GPA didn't impress anyone. Then again, neither did Steve Jobs's 2.65 GPA in high school. Not everyone can be Bill Gates and have a 4.0. I finally figured out how to excel at selling because I realized quickly that my livelihood depended on it. I had to find a way to excel, or I was doomed to a life of mediocrity. So I studied books by experts and learned from those who were excelling.

I found the keys to success, and I have *never* stopped looking for new ideas to help me be even better. Now I am fortunate to spend my time helping thousands of others find victory. So, all I'll say is, if I can do it, anybody can do it.

I've teamed up with my fellow sales Jedi Jeremy Miner to show you that today's sales slayers don't just sell, they help customers buy by *thinking like a buyer* instead of acting like a seller. You'll see that it's not only successful but it's actually fun.

Jeremy Miner

I am Jeremy Miner. I pioneered 7th Level, an internationally recognized sales training company and its methodology that, to date, has helped more than 439,000 salespeople and counting in 158 different industries achieve exceptional results.

I wasn't born a superstar salesperson. I was born in Arkansas and grew up in a town in the middle of Missouri that had fewer than eight hundred people in it. What made the difference for me was that I developed and mastered persuasion skills that work *with* human behavior, not against it.

Over seventeen years ago, as a broke, struggling, burned-out college student, I was barely making a living with door-to-door sales. The company would take us out in a van, drop us off in some dodgy neighborhoods, and say, "Go make some sales, and we will pick you up after dark!" My initial thought was it was going to be easy because that's what the recruiter had told me. They gave us a script and a few books by the "gurus," and we were on our way!

After around six to eight weeks, because of all the doors slammed in my face and hardly any sales, I got to a point where I thought maybe selling wasn't for me. At the same time, I was studying behavioral science and human psychology at Utah Valley University. There, I specialized in neuroscience or the study of the brain, how humans make decisions, and the intricate dance of persuasion.

Just as I was about to quit, one day I was driving down the road with the sales manager and he popped in a Tony Robbins CD, and Tony said something like,

"Most people fail for the simple reason they don't learn the right skills necessary to succeed."

A light bulb immediately went off in my head, that maybe, just maybe, what I'm learning from my company and from the OGs who I called "Old Sales Gurus" were not the right skills. Maybe they were just outdated. There's no ageism here; it's just that the skills being passed around were old and expired.

With all these questions starting to swirl around in my head, I also started looking into these so-called gurus' actual sales experience, and I thought, *If these guys know all this stuff and are so great at selling, why weren't they making seven figures a year as a salesperson in their jobs before they started a company and became a so-called sales guru?* Because my goal at the time was to make seven figures a year somehow, so why not do it as a salesperson?! And how could they teach me those types of skills if they never got to that level themselves as a salesperson?

So here I was learning these traditional selling techniques, but at the same time, I was learning from behavioral science that the most persuasive way to sell is to get others to persuade themselves—the exact opposite of what my company and all the "sales gurus" were teaching me. Instead of sticking to the traditional selling techniques, I decided to take a massive leap outside my comfort zone to learn the most persuasive way to sell so you make way more sales. And I did. It wasn't easy, but I did it.

I came up with some of what's known as neuro-emotional persuasion questions (NEPQs) and my sales doubled. But I still didn't know all the right questions to ask, or when and how to ask them. I didn't have a structure. I was winging it, and I knew I was still losing sales that I should have been making.

Then I got a little diabolical—cue evil snicker here—and came up with a slightly devious plan in which I would go out and find a sales training program, because in my mind, surely there had to be one that had *all* these elements of behavioral science, with the magical phrases and questions I needed to ask to get my prospects to persuade themselves in an easy step-by-step sequence.

After I bought *every* sales training course known to man, went to every sales training conference, read hundreds of books on selling, and spent tens of thousands of dollars on sales training from the gurus, that dream course that I thought was out there, well, it just didn't exist. What an epic buzzkill. I decided right then and there that I was going to have to master this myself.

I was going to incorporate everything I was learning from behavioral science and human psychology into selling and I would create this course myself if I had to. Wow, that's really inspiring, right? No, it actually really sucked. It took twelve years of trial, error, eye-rolls, and fighting the desire to pull my hair out of my head or pour hot tar in my eyes before I figured it all out. And even now, I'm still learning. But through it all, I created a book of phrases and questions that skyrocketed my sales career, but more importantly, the careers of the salespeople I trained.

It has now become my divine mission and purpose to share my Jedi master sales tips and train you so you can learn how to communicate and sell to today's modern consumer.

How We Met

How our sales partnership came about is a pretty interesting story. I challenged my team to find fifty top sales trainers to interview on our new podcast, *Closers are Losers*, and, well, enter Jerry Acuff!

Until I interviewed Jerry, I was unimpressed. Because the people I spoke to were viewed as top sales trainers, I thought they would be up to date with modern-day selling skills. Unfortunately, I quickly discovered most weren't. It was like listening to a bad cover song on repeat, but with the wrong lyrics.

Their advice didn't vibe well with today's information-at-your-fingertips prospect. It was like sales pitch Ambien. I was falling asleep. I needed a Red Bull. No one was saying anything new, that is, until Jerry walked in. We talked for a good ten minutes before I brought him on the show, and I was amazed at his knowledge and understanding of how to use human behavior in the sales process. It was a bona fide sales banger, a hit, as opposed to the tired, overplayed, auto-tuned one-hit wonders.

By the time the show finished, I realized I'd finally swiped right. I knew I had found someone I could identify with, someone who knew where I came from, someone from whom I could learn and grow, and someone with whom I could work without it feeling like work. That is exactly how *all* your sales calls should be.

With years of experience in the sales world, we are dedicated to helping others reach the same level of success. We share a selling approach that guarantees the greatest likelihood of success using someone's current ability to enhance skills and build trust with prospects that help them persuade themselves.

Our collaboration on this book gives you the benefit of our combined expertise in a craft that is widely done in America, but most of the time, not done very well. Going from zero to one is always the most challenging step. But the good news is that you're already there! You've already decided that you want to learn new skills, and you're ready to master this exciting, ever-evolving universe!

Chapter 1

The Biggest Problem in Sales

People don't know what they want until you show it to them.
—Steve Jobs

Sales isn't rocket science, but it *is* neuroscience, and that's what some frustrated colleagues in the biz fail to grasp. Sales is a relationship-based role-play between the buyer and the salesperson, but far too often, we the salespeople are playing the wrong parts, acting like sellers when we should really be thinking (there's that neuroscience!) like buyers.

What do you believe are some of the biggest problems in sales? Not having great leads? Not being enthusiastic enough? Needing better product knowledge, learning to close more effectively, learning to challenge your customers? Maybe you believe it's some or all of the above or something not mentioned.

If you're looking to increase your sales, you have to understand the problem is not your leads. It's not your enthusiasm. It's not your product knowledge. It's not that you don't listen to enough personal development podcasts or you're not motivated enough. It has nothing to do with those things at all. You need to let go of all these beliefs. Leveling up in this world requires you to clean the slate and, for a change, suspend your stagnant sales beliefs. Beliefs won't get you anywhere. What you need is the cold, hard truth. Are you ready for it? Buckle up.

The truth is your sales may not be where you want them to be due to several problems that you haven't even uncovered yet. There could be things you are doing, or more importantly, things you're saying that are far more likely to cause your prospects to turn away and not buy your solution. After all, if they don't buy from you, then you can't solve their problems, right?

The premise of what we are going to share in this book will present you with that "Aha!" eureka moment, that proverbial light bulb, only this time it's a hipster Edison bulb or whatever the latest lighting fad is these days. In other words, it's modern, it's what we're using now, and it's something that, unlike the ubiquitous hipster Edison bulb, will never go out of style. It may have to adapt to the times, but the basic premise is purposeful and timeless. And not only that but the anxiety that's been weighing you down will also dim down and disappear, freeing you to master your sales craft into colossal success!

Here's the rub: you have to trade in your old sales techniques like you did your last smartphone. It's so last decade. Consumers are barely recognizable these days and have drastically changed. They've upgraded their operating systems to work compatibly with the times.

They're not just Instagram filters smoothing out the rough edges. Although the stereotype of a pushy used car salesman has survived the disco, new wave, punk, '80s synth pop, grunge, and Auto-Tune eras, the way to adequately address and eradicate these misconceptions and predictable sales resistance has changed.

The way to connect with people has changed. And, whether you are a child of the '60s or a millennial Deadhead who used to follow Phish, you know that times have also changed. Trust has always had to be earned, but today's consumer has become more cautious and skeptical than ever before. Yes, it's exhausting and at times exasperating, especially living in a society of experts aided by nothing but Google, but what's consistent is that consumers do not want to be talked *at* and sold *to*, they want to be talked to, asked, heard, and most importantly, understood.

The biggest problem in sales is the problem you don't know you have. Wait, what? Read that again because it is remarkably powerful and true. It also speaks to the absolute necessity of self-awareness. Cluelessness and a subway token won't get you very far. The key to all growth and development is self-awareness. If you don't know what the biggest problem you have is, you're in a real bind, and in sales, that bind is the equivalent of a cold call hang up or a door slammed in your face. If you don't know what the problem is, how can you fix it? You can't. But as soon as you identify the problem, you can and *will* change your situation.

No one aspires to become a professional most associated with the adjectives "sleazy," "aggressive," "annoying," and "slick." Think about your best teachers. They were inspiring, motivating, and thought-provoking, right? Great salespeople are like your favorite teachers. They inform, involve, engage, and provoke thought. They interact; they connect. And as high tech as things are these days, sales, like school, is best done person to person and not virtually (yet sometimes that is the only viable opportunity). It's essential that every salesperson is in step with the way *people want to be sold to*. It's not about having the right product. It's about having the right method *and* the right solution or product. As Jeffrey Gitomer, who writes and lectures on sales, customer loyalty, and personal development, says in his book *21.5 Unbreakable Laws of Selling*, "People hate to be sold, but they love to buy."

It's called the sales *business* for a reason; we all want our products and services to go viral, but that's not going to happen with old-school approaches. It's like taking a Betamax tape (Google alert for millennials and Zoomers) and trying to load it into a DVD player, or worse, trying to convert it to a streamable MOV or MP4 file. It just doesn't work, and while you're scrounging to make it work anyway, your customers have long moved on and made their purchase elsewhere. It's easy to get burned out and want to quit. We've all been there at some point. We want to help you avoid this at all costs.

If this is where you currently are, you can begin doing something about it ASAP. Cue that Tony Robbins quote here: "Most people fail in life because they don't learn the right skills necessary to succeed." Too many salespeople today are not using a sales structure—a step-by-step system that works for them and worse yet, it doesn't work for their customers or prospects.

Before we provide you with the blueprint for selling excellence in today's era, we need to discuss some of the biggest problems in sales to better understand why these strategies are outdated and not nearly as successful as they may have once been.

Problem 1: The Definition of Sales Is Inconsistent

If you ask fifty salespeople to define selling, you will likely get fifty different answers, and in this case, that's forty-nine too many. The correct definition of selling is probably best approached as *one* definition. Why is this important? Because your beliefs drive your behavior. If you don't have the right mindset and the right definition of sales, you will not have the skills and tools needed to succeed. You can bring a baseball bat to a football game, but you or your team won't score any touchdowns with it and you'll probably be kicked out.

Contrary to what you might have read in books or seen in movies, the true essence of selling is *not* about convincing, persuading, manipulating, or pushing someone into doing something you want them to do. Selling is quite the opposite. The definition of selling is almost like a Disney movie plot: it's about believing in yourself and making others, in this case, the customer, believe in you too. And while those beliefs may seem magical, at the end of the day or the movie, they're really just elements of human nature driving behavior and not Tinkerbell's pixie dust.

If you were a contestant on *Jeopardy!* and the host (RIP Alex Trebek), whoever they decided on after all the drama, read the following answer: "A profession in which the goal is for you to close that sale so you can make some cash," and you buzzed in with, "What is sales?" You'd be wrong and out of money. The answer would be "What is the incorrect definition of sales?"

You see, your primary goal in sales is to interact with your potential customer and discover whether there's a sale to be made in the first place. Let's repeat that because it is so important. *Your primary goal in sales is to interact with a potential customer and discover whether there's a sale to be made or not.*

While we won't go into extensive detail about the former models, we believe knowing what doesn't work will give you the clarity you need to recognize what does work.

Problem 2: Former Models Are Outdated

The first sales training program was created in 1884 by John H. Patterson. His employees memorized scripts, introducing door-to-door sales to local businesses. It was a novel concept for its time, and remember, TV wasn't invented until

1927, so perhaps people welcomed strangers knocking at their door hawking fancy new products.

A little over a decade later, in 1898, the AIDA model was created by Elias St. Elmo Lewis. His method stood for Attention, Interest, Desire, and Action. It was adopted by American advertising and has been used ever since. The AIDA model was used to attract customers to purchase their products because twenty-plus years ago, the salesperson was the bridge between consumer and company. The company would dispatch the salesperson to educate the public about its products or services. Besides radio and TV, this was the only way the consumer could learn about the business.

Today, as you know, anyone can learn anything with the click of a button. Armchair experts are as ubiquitous as Jennifer Lopez and Ben Affleck on their second go-around. So, if everyone has instant access to information, why is this method still widely used today? The thing is, while the information is available, you still have to *understand* it to activate it. You can read a WebMD article to diagnose your hangnail, but the medical terms for hangnail may go over your head, or worse, through your toe. Modern salespeople don't have an untrained eye, but an inaccurately trained one.

The former eras of selling were crafted from the first sales model and only had minor tweaks, which, as behavioral science has shown, are not very persuasive to today's sophisticated, information-aged buyers, who are used to getting what they want instantly. While Pa may have gladly bought a new fiddle from a door-to-door salesman on *Little House on the Prairie*, the antiquated methods of sales can be very unsettling or downright inexplicable to today's consumers because the information they think they need is available at the click of a mouse or the tap and swipe of a smartphone.

Here are some of the greatest hits of old-timey, tired sales techniques:

- The assumptive sale
- ABC (always be closing)
- Feel, felt, found
- The trial close
- The demonstration close

- Be relentless
- Chase the sale
- Be enthusiastic about your product and solutions
- Accept rejection as a normal part of selling
- And one that's heard as often in sales as Kool and the Gang's "Celebration" is heard at bar mitzvahs and weddings, "It's a numbers game; get as many nos as you can to get to a yes."

Problem 3: Pressuring Prospects Isn't Effective

Let's start with the high-drama boiler-room selling, where you psychologically pressure your prospects into the purchase by promising puppies, rainbows, and unicorns. Appealing to one's fear, greed, and pride to sell your product or service is why salespeople get a bad rap. It's gross and, while it may have worked briefly for *The Wolf of Wall Street* protagonist Jordan Belfort, he ended up broke and in prison. It's the antithesis of what works.

Even Belfort eventually admitted it, saying, "I got greedy. . . . Greed is not good. Ambition is good, passion is good. Passion prospers." (Shh, don't tell Gordon Gekko).

The brutal boiler-room method of manipulation and posturing is passé. If you cross the line of being persistent, overly assumptive, and too domineering, you risk creating resistance in the long run and coming across as desperate and even unethical, not passionate! High-pressure selling is harassment, and it's history.

In 1973, best-selling author the late Joe Girard received the Guinness World Record for the most cars sold in one year. In his book, *How to Sell Anything to Anybody*, he says if prospects mention they've recently been on vacation somewhere, he'll say that he's been there too—even if he hasn't. Last we heard, that's called lying.

Girard wasn't authentic or honest with his prospects. As an attempt to "connect" with them, he misrepresented himself and downright lied to garner favor. There is one thing that you should know about Girard. He hasn't sold a car since 1977! He quit the business almost four decades ago to teach others how to lie . . . er, sell. His selling methods seemed to work in the mid-'70s, but today, he would be fully exposed, dare we say shamed, on social media and probably stack up plenty of bad reviews on Yelp.

Did his methods work in the past? Of course they did! But I bet if you plugged your circa 2010 smartphone into the charger, that would work too. We're not saying the age-old tricks don't have merit. They can still hold their own, but they are a bit wonky. They are not as efficient, and we can show you a better way.

Problem 4: They *Need* to Want It

Born in the '70s, *consultative selling,* like so many Gen Xers, came into its own in the '80s and involves listening to the needs, wants, and goals of a prospective client as a doctor would their patient. It requires you to ask logical, qualifying questions to find out the needs of the client, such as, "What are the three biggest problems your company is facing right now?" or "How many robot dogs can your 3D printer churn out in an hour?"

What is the biggest problem with asking questions like these? Logical questions elicit logical answers, and while we love logic (who doesn't?), do people buy on logic or emotion? The OG of corporate training, Dale Carnegie, said 85 percent of our decisions are emotional and 15 percent are logical. Also, unless you're on a game show, people don't tend to love interrogations and answering a litany of questions.

This way of selling requires the salesperson to focus on selling the solution, *not* the product. Let's go back to the guy with the robot dog-generating 3D printer. Say his problem involves software and you're selling printer ink. You had no idea he had a software problem and that he's not necessarily in the market for ink. Or is he?

You can't assume the customer wants what you have to offer and just walk in there and expect an order. You know what would have saved you a trip to the doghouse? Research. Perhaps that research would identify a need for robot dog red ink, but you won't know if you don't dig.

One of the biggest drawbacks of needs-based selling, which is what consultative selling embodies, is that the person you are interacting with may not want to solve their problem. Just because you identify a need for a prospect doesn't mean they have any urgency to fill that need.

Neil Rackham, the author of *SPIN Selling*, teaches that you must ask questions to find your clients' needs. What type of selling do you think this is? It's still needs-based selling that implies that the prospects know their problems, but most of our customers don't even know their real problems when you first talk to them. Maybe the robot dog red ink would somehow help assuage that pesky software problem, but first you need to find out what that problem is.

Asking someone what keeps them awake at night or what problems they are experiencing will not get you the results you are looking for when it comes to selling, and it may get you TMI. Sure, it shows you have an interest in them, but how helpful are your questions? They're certainly loaded questions, eliciting answers that may have absolutely nothing to do with what you're selling, but you aren't likely to get far if the questions you're asking aren't exposing the actual issues that need to be addressed. You may, however, walk out of there with an honorary degree in marriage counseling, parenting, or nutrition. Although our primary goal is to obtain pertinent information to uncover whether they have problems our products or services can actually solve, some of the things we hear or learn can actually help with relationship building, so it's a win-win.

If it's true that selling slam dunks occur when we have customers willingly conversing with us, then we need to keep that ball in play by either saying something worthy of a bumper sticker, a meme, a retweet, or a comparison to a historic genius, or by asking exceptional questions. Taking the focus away from you and centering on the prospect is only genuine if you do both or either.

By spewing out a standard list of questions, it can easily come off as scripted and forced. Were you taught to ask these questions? Are you still currently using them in your sales process? Throw them out the door. They are cliché, surface level, and snoozeworthy.

Problem 5: Consumers and Times Have Changed

Today's consumers are wiser, more informed, more prepared, less patient, and less trustworthy than ever, and they come armed with an overload of information that can zap any ill-prepared salesperson into irrelevancy. Thank you, Google. But wait! Don't blame search engines for your slacking.

We are *much* more persuasive when we interact and discover from each other, which is why we can show you what *actually* works and the scientific data behind it. People most often buy emotionally and defend their decisions logically. If you aren't helping the consumer engage with their emotions, you're missing a huge opportunity.

So many salespeople who use traditional selling techniques assume that because the lead has requested information to be sent to them, they are eager and ready to buy. Some of you may have even requested more information on the aforementioned 3D-printed robot dog but does it mean you're going to replace Rover? Hardly (right?).

If you haven't learned by now, never *ever* assume a prospect wants to buy just because they requested some information. Think about how many times you have been burned because you called back what you thought was a hot lead, jumped right into your pitch, and then ten minutes later the prospect says, "I need to think it over," and you never hear from them again!

Customers today are smarter and more cautious than ever before. They can feel if you are too attached to making the sale when talking to them. They can tell if you care too much about the sale (which means that you care solely about the sale, not about solving their problems). That idea alone is the epitome of sales selfishness. It's often driven by your sales manager and leaders who have just not yet learned how to use human behavior to their advantage in the sales process. It's just a numbers game to them, and they churn through prospects to make a few sales.

Your prospects can sniff this out very quickly on you, the salesperson. Their defense mechanisms are triggered daily by pushy, needy salespeople trying to force feed them with the sales biz equivalent of empty calories and nutrient-free fluff, or worse than that, potato chips made with Olestra—Google it at your own risk. Because you aspire to climb to the top in sales, you must lose this approach immediately when dealing with the modern-day consumer/buyer.

To illustrate how our New Model is different, try not to fall asleep reading this transcript between prospect and salesperson. In this scenario, an average salesperson who uses traditional selling techniques is calling someone who requested information from a digital marketing service's website.

Prospect: *"Hi, this is Alex."*
Average Salesperson: *"Hi, Alex. My name is John Smith. You requested my company, XYZ Digital Marketing, to send you a packet of information on*

the marketing strategies we offer to businesses like yours. Do you have two minutes to talk now?"

Prospect: *"Sure . . ."* (hesitantly)

You follow? Do you think the prospect believes that the salesperson will only take two minutes of their time? What do you think they're thinking at this point?

Average Salesperson: *"OK, well, like I said, my name is John, and I am a digital strategist with XYZ Digital Marketing. We help a lot of companies like yours save a ton of money by effectively implementing strategies to save you money and increase your bottom line."*

Prospect: *"How do you do that? We already have a company that does that for us."*

Average Salesperson: *"Yeah, I know your business has gotten very complicated."*

Notice how this salesperson is assuming instead of asking whether it has become complicated. Also, notice that this statement doesn't involve them in the process. Think about what's probably going on in the prospect's mind. What would be going through yours besides z's? How would you respond?

Average Salesperson: *"I know there are a lot of choices out there, and marketing dollars are all over the place today, and it's extremely costly to you."*

The salesperson is still assuming it's costly without asking whether it is. This triggers more sales resistance.

Prospect: *"Well, actually, it's not that costly at all. We have really developed a plan where last year we saved 32 percent from the same marketing we did the year before."*

Average Salesperson: *"Well, if I could show you a way to get that cost down even more, when could you chat with me for fifteen minutes this week? I know we can save you more money than your current company."*

The words *"If I could show you"* immediately puts the focus on whom? Yep. You guessed it—the salesperson. If you continue to bring the focus back to you instead of keeping your attention on the prospect, you'll be greeted with rejection nine times out of ten.

What happens now is that the salesperson is forced to go into sales pitch mode with logical facts to support themselves and their solution. This is also when a salesperson becomes extremely self-justified and feels they have to defend their product or service. As salespeople, all of us have been there, but when you ask the questions we're about to teach you, you won't have to resort to drastic measures.

Wants-based selling is the better way to sell. Most people say they need a new car, vacation, or someone to clean their house. When was the last time you heard someone say, "I want a new pair of shoes?" OK, wait, lots of people want new shoes. How about, "I want a new broom?"

People in all industries and walks of life ordinarily justify purchases as being something they need; however, that's not usually the case. Most of us buy what we want, not what we need. If we only bought what we needed, Target probably would have filed Chapter 11 by now.

The traditional selling models have salespeople lulled into believing that customers are buying because they need what we have to offer. We are trying to meet the needs of our customers instead of focusing on meeting their wants. If customers made purchase decisions based solely on needs, the only booming biz anywhere would be the place printing "Out of Business" signs.

Keep in mind the prospect may need your solution, but they may not want it now. Many buyers don't truly know what they want, but they think they do. As Steve Jobs said, "People don't know what they want until you show it to them."

Traditionally, salespeople have not pursued the things a customer might want. While they believe the customer is always right, the customer may not be aware of what the company has to offer, and the questioning skill of the salesperson can lead them to see that we can solve problems they didn't even know they had. Good questions force people to think, they promote dialogue, and they're an ideal way to learn how your customers think.

Problem 6: The Old Method Triggers Sales Resistance

The Challenger sales method is based on research published in a 2011 book that says you'll experience a sales boost if you challenge customers' assumptions or beliefs by pinpointing flaws or untruths in them, thus opening the door to offer a better solution. This method leans on delivering insight about an unknown problem they didn't even know they had, with the salesperson jumping in to save the day with a solution to that newly unearthed "problem."

It can be hard to challenge without making the customer feel challenged. This requires skills many training teams do not teach well. Theoretically, this approach can work, but it is difficult to do well because at its core it assumes the salesperson will have a degree of expertise that the prospect doesn't have. That is a big ask of a salesperson who may not have serious and deep knowledge of that customer's business and their uniqueness as an organization.

Think of the door-to-door exterminator selling his revolutionary plant-based, bug-zapping product—the one who swiped a cluster of mosquito eggs you never knew you had from the top of your doorbell as you opened the door. Did you even know you had that issue, or did you think that, prior to this hands-on, unplanned, improvisational demo, your peskiest problem was the salesman himself?

People rarely fully realize the problems they have or even know they have something they need to solve, and they're often unaware of its urgency. Sometimes they don't fully grasp the negative or positive consequences of what will happen if they don't solve their problems, issues, or challenges.

Through your questioning ability, you'll be able to help them clearly see their problem, and maybe two, three, or four other problems they also have that they didn't even realize they had before talking to you. Mosquitoes be gone!

Pay attention! Yes, now, and especially when you approach your prospect. You can't have a skilled conversation without listening. When you haven't had a skilled conversation where you truly try to discover the entirety of the customer's issues, you can neither understand nor discover the true problem, and the customer can see right through you, straight to the salesperson standing behind you armed with these skills and ready to make the sale *you* were supposed to make.

It's also the case that to do this type of selling as it's taught, it means we must have unique insight that the customer doesn't have about their own business. While you're not expected to be some all-knowing mind reader, this can be problematic for many salespeople because, often, the customer knows far more detail about their own business than we do.

All of these former sales eras have one thing in common: they unintentionally, but almost certainly, build sales resistance. Oof, resistance is sales kryptonite—a sales slayer in the murderous, not victorious, sense of the word. The New Model of Selling removes resistance from the equation and revives your bottom line. Now that's irresistible, right?

Our experience as sales experts who have studied this science for decades shows that the vast majority of very successful salespeople today do not sell based on the golden olden days. Instead, they've adapted to a new way of interacting and creating far more opportunities to genuinely solve people's problems. Next up, world peace. Just kidding. Well, maybe we're not!

Selling is no longer about being challenging, being aggressive, and pushing people into doing something you want them to do. It's about breaking down why people think the way they do and helping them think for themselves. You cannot change what your customer thinks if you don't know what they think in the first place.

Problem 7: Trust Has Died

"When salesmen are doing well, there is pressure upon them to begin doing better, for fear they may start doing worse," wrote *Catch-22* author Joseph Heller in *Something Happened*. And although diamonds are created under pressure, human beings have never liked being pressurized. While some create diamonds under it, others undoubtedly crumble and end up with cubic zirconia. People like to make their own decisions and have always wanted choices. Have you ever googled a white T-shirt on Amazon? You'll be scrolling for hours looking at variations of the same white tee. A plethora of choices aside, people prefer to do biz with those whom they trust.

John Maxwell, business leader and author of The 21 Irrefutable Laws of Leadership, says, "All things being equal, people do business with people they like." Frankly, equal or not equal, we don't think people do business with you because they like you (no offense). Rather they do business with you because they trust you. That trust is built through your questioning ability that causes the prospect to view you as the trusted expert. Put simply, they buy because they trust you're going to get them the results they want.

Times, in case you haven't noticed, have changed drastically. None of the tactics above will help you reach your *full* potential. If you want to move past your goals, you have to change too. Far too many prospects assume salespeople will be biased and focused only on the "sale" before the conversation even begins. Saying "trust me" isn't enough anymore. In fact, saying "trust me" is the death knell of modern-day sales. If you have to say it, your customer is likely to immediately do the opposite.

Show them, don't tell them. This is a very visual-oriented society. Everything has a GIF, a meme, a viral video, or an entirely too long reality series that should have ended years ago. But alas, it is what it is. The modern salesperson knows that trust is paramount in sales. That being said, trust is also even harder to gain in this age of armchair experts and instant gratification.

People have instant access to any information they need about your company. They know all about your products or services and your price points. They know who your competitors are. They know how long you've been in business and what your office building looks like on Google Maps. They know everything about you by doing a quick search on their smartphone. They know what you did last summer. Creepy, isn't it? Yes and no. It's good to have an informed customer. It's not good to have one who thinks they know everything about you because of a Google search.

Information has transformed over the last few decades with a massive increase in channels, opinions, voices, and, for better or for worse, the proliferation of social media and the internet. With so many different opinions from experts, people who think they're experts, and influencers, people seek out information and judge their credibility independently.

Because we have reduced phone conversations to messages that people barely listen to, messages to texts, and texts to symbols and emojis, modern-day salespeople not only have a higher burden of credibility but far less time to build it. Stir all of these things together with factors ranging from more information to more complex products, and you have the new digitally fueled skeptic because we are now in "post-trust era" America, a term coined by Michael Maslansky, one of corporate America's leading communications and research strategists.

In a 2019 Pew Research Center poll[1], a whopping 71 percent said they think interpersonal confidence has worsened in the past twenty years. As Edelman's 2021 Trust Barometer[2], which has been measuring public trust or lack thereof for over twenty years, points out, people don't know who to believe anymore. Trust has been eroded by many factors, but the bottom line is, people especially don't trust salespeople. But, breaking news, water is wet. They also don't trust their government, but again, water, wet. Sadly, some people don't even trust their own family.

As David Brooks in *The Atlantic* said, "We are living in the age of that disappointment . . . this has produced a crisis of faith, across society but especially among the young. It has produced a crisis of trust." And unlike your typical midlife crisis, you can't go out and buy a sports car to regain that trust, though there is no shortage of salespeople who will certainly recommend doing so. But put that Lambo in neutral for a minute.

According to another survey conducted by the Pew Research Center, 40 percent of baby boomers (born 1946–1964) and 37 percent of those in the Silent Generation (1928–1945) believed that people could be trusted. However, when they surveyed younger people, they found this significantly dropped. Pew noted that "around three-quarters (73%) of U.S. adults under 30 believe people 'just look out for themselves' most of the time."[3] Pew, indeed. We have our work cut out for us, to say the least.

And this trust crisis seeps into everything we do. Gone are the days when salespeople could pick up the phone and call a company that would take the call and listen. Gone are the days when you could sell your benefits and features, tell your story, give presentations, create a vision, and talk down your competitors, hoping to build credibility with your product or service.

No need to curl up into your safe space over it, though. If you want to sell in the modern world, you can start by doing these three things:

1. Learn to eliminate sales resistance.
2. Focus on the customer.
3. Get the customer to think for themselves and question their current way of thinking.

Accomplishing this holy troika of modern-era sales success will require you to *unlearn* the majority of traditional selling techniques you've been taught and have an open mind to begin doing things differently because times have changed, so it's time for the way we approach sales to change. Spoiler alert: you *can* do this.

If you'd like to learn how to get your prospects to sell themselves rather than you chasing them down to try to convince them, you must step outside your comfort zone, say "Bye, Felicia," to the traditional selling beliefs and techniques that are holding you back, and learn to be truly customer-focused at all times.

Jerry's company Delta Point isn't called Delta because of his frequent flier miles. DELTA is an acronym that encapsulates the New Model of great sales processes, standing for Develop, Engage, Learn, Tell, and Ask.

1. **D**evelop prospective customers' interest so they are willing to hear you out.
2. **E**ngage customers in a meaningful dialogue.
3. **L**earn the prospect's situation/problem/challenge.
4. **T**ell your story after you clearly understand that your product or service is a fit for their situation, problem, or challenge.
5. **A**sk for a commitment—that is, when a commitment is appropriate.

But one step at a time here.

Since we've identified the biggest problems in sales and why these former models no longer work very well, it's almost time to jump into getting past the gatekeeper manning the velvet ropes and into the VIP section so you can get one step closer to achieving sales greatness for you, your company, your family, and *especially* your potential customers. But before we do that, it's important to differentiate between sales myths and sales realities.

Chapter 2

Sales Myths vs. Sales Realities

The great enemy of the truth is very often not the lie—deliberate, contrived, and dishonest—but the myth—persistent, persuasive, and unrealistic.
—John F. Kennedy

I f you've ever watched a reality show, you know that the word *reality* should be in ironic quotes, considering that much of it is anything but reality and just scripted drivel designed to fuel drama. While it may be mindless fun to keep up with a family that's as real as a knockoff Birkin bag sold on Canal Street, it's not real life, and neither are the old-school, common sales beliefs that have now become cliché; these "beliefs" are really just myths that are not at all based in today's reality.

Let's take that tried-and-not-so-true "Selling is a numbers game." Is this your reality? Do you believe that selling is just a numbers game and you have to call prospects over and over again just to get a few sales? Or a better question to ask if you aren't sure is, is that mantra working for you? If it was, you probably wouldn't be reading this book right now and you'd be on a selling spree.

Just like an internet sleuth discovered that HGTV fave *House Hunters* wasn't 100 percent real, the following dispels some of the most hackneyed sales myths out there.

Sales Myth #1: Selling Is a Numbers Game

Selling can indeed be a numbers game, that is, if all you know are traditional selling techniques. You can call people incessantly, becoming a borderline stalker, and go through hundreds of calls a day just to make a few sales and eke out a living. You can also chase them down until they listen to you, just so that they can come up with an excuse to get rid of you, hoping they don't take out a restraining order on you first. Good times, no? Not so much.

Where did the "numbers game" concept come from? Hard to say, but probably, several decades ago, a sales manager somewhere told his salespeople that selling is a "numbers game" to make them feel better about themselves after facing constant rejection 95 percent of the time. Alas, that myth's number is up.

Wouldn't it be nice to skip all that work and bypass all the objections and rejection? In the post-trust era, with trust being at its lowest point ever, it's no longer about the *quantity* of calls you make or how many contacts you reach. It's about the *quality* of your conversations and your ability to bring out their emotions by asking deep questions. It's about how good you are at creating *trust*.

It's about how good you are at detaching yourself from the *expectation* of making a sale. This allows you to become open to your potential customers. You'll learn what their problems are, what's causing those problems, and how those problems are affecting them, and you'll be able to see whether your solution will help them.

When you have these conversations in a calm, conversational voice as opposed to the typical sales pitch, you will automatically attract your potential customers to you like a magnet. Why? Because, for the first time in a long time, someone is genuinely interested in them and what they are looking for. This is the antithesis of what they feel about number gamers a.k.a. typical salespeople. They feel your intent, and they'll start to lean on you because you've become the trusted expert, the authority in the market, numero uno.

How would you feel if you were no longer met with defiance and resistance right from the start of each call you made to your prospects? What would that do for you personally? What would it do for you financially? Your answers to these questions aren't myths. They can become your reality!

Sales Myth #2: Rejection Is Just a Part of Sales

What is the greatest fear you and other salespeople have that holds you back from making calls and talking to prospects about your products/services? It's the fear of rejection, right?

Have you ever considered that if you get anxious and panic about meeting prospects, cold calling, or calling your leads to the point where you can't talk to your prospects that something may be wrong? Do you need to get pumped up before every meeting with prospective clients, or do you drag your feet before making those calls? Have you considered it could be the way you are communicating or think you have to communicate that is causing this problem? Do you like being rejected by your prospects? How does it make you feel? Why do you believe that rejection is just something you have to accept in selling? So many questions, we know, but they need to be answered.

You accept the rejection because that's what you have been told will happen—that rejection just comes with the territory, right? What if many of your prospects reject you because *you* are the one triggering the rejection by the way you are communicating with them? What if you could learn what those triggers are that cause you to get objections from your prospects and ultimately be rejected so that you can eliminate them from your sales conversations?

Swiss psychiatrist Carl Jung had a great point when he said, "The best political, social, and spiritual work we can do is to withdraw the projection of our shadow onto others." And we here are no psychiatrists, but we'd also like to add sales work to that list.

There are two types of rejection; there's the flat-out in your face, "I'm not interested," and there's a less painful form in which your prospect has looked at your solution and determined that it doesn't fit their needs. The second one can be disappointing, but it doesn't necessarily feel personal or sting so much.

But about the first one. You have probably been told time and time again that rejection is part of selling and to expect it and get over it, that you just have to have thick skin. By now, your skin is so thick, you don't need a dermo, you need a vet specializing in reptiles. However, all of that is just nonsense You can actually eliminate a significant amount of rejection. You don't need mind games, mental tricks, or personal development guru CDs. When you master the New Model sales techniques, you'll learn how to diffuse the cause of rejection like Shazam used his lightning power to zap cash out of a bank machine.

Sales Myth #3: You Need to Be Enthusiastic about Your Product/Service

If the customer sees that you're excited, they'll get excited too. This one's hilarious. It's like that joke or meme that has you rolling on the floor in tears of laughter and then crickets when you show the person next to you what you thought was so riotous and they just look at you like you're nuts. Whatever you do, never, ever assume that your excitement and enthusiasm will rub off on your clients. Their motivations for buying something or making a change will vary from person to person. When you approach someone with too much external enthusiasm, they will do one of two things.

They'll likely either withdraw from you because you have overwhelmed them, freaked them out, or totally turned them off to you and tell you they'll think about it only to disappear quicker than Don Julio tequila at an open bar, or they get defensive, throw out objections, and flat out reject you and what you're offering and introduce you to their good friend, the door.

Sales Myth #4: The Sale Is Lost at the End of the Sale

Perhaps you've spent a lot of time with a potential customer, and you've done everything right, but then, as you wait for the contract or final approval, it just doesn't happen, and though we have issues at the USPS, no, it didn't get lost in the mail. It didn't even get lost on the Pony Express. It just never got to that point. Why is that? These days, the sale is no longer lost at the end of the sale. It's now lost at the beginning of the sale. The sale is lost at "Hello." Yep, you lost them at hello. But how? Why? It's got nothing to do with your perfume or cologne.

Here's an example.

When they make a cold call, most salespeople would say something like this:

> *"Hello, my name is Shelly Levene. I'm with XYZ Company, and the reason why I called you today is . . . "* and then Shelly goes into trying to explain his product or service if he hasn't already been cut off by the prospect.

Sound familiar?

What do you think goes on in the prospect's mind at this point? *"Ah, it's just another salesperson trying to sell me something."* It's the classic sales pitch. And it's over at "Hello" because we unintentionally yet inadvertently triggered sales resistance. In human psychology, this is called a schema, a cognitive framework or concept that helps us interpret information that oftentimes can contribute to stereotypes such as: *"Yikes, this guy is a used car salesman. I'll be polite, but I will tune him out."*

Sales Myth #5: If You Assume the Sale, They Will Buy

Rest in peace, rest in power(less) assumptive selling. Yep, in today's world, assumptive selling is dead. Yet, like Elvis and Tupac, some sales gurus insist it's alive and well and living in some secret sales city only to emerge from time to time to hit Walmart. Why? People don't like change. Salespeople are still taught to assume the sale, always be closing, and always look for ways to close the sale. These sayings have been passed down by the old sales gurus like hand-me-downs and, well, they just don't fit anymore. We've grown out of them.

As obvious as a piece of spinach stuck in between your front teeth after lunch, your potential client can immediately tell that you're assuming the sale. And instead of subtly tapping their own front teeth to clue you in on that, they'll just hit you back with a flurry of objections.

But you can't blame them for that pesky sales spinach giving off the illusion that you are missing a front tooth and blocking you from a sale. It's your fault. You are the one causing the rejection by the way you were originally taught to communicate.

Let's say that you get to the end of your presentation and you're assuming the sale and you say, *"In whose name should the contract be? What's your phone number, what's your address, what are your bank details . . . ?"* You just shot off some serious sales kryptonite with that one.

Then the customer does what nine out of ten times? They'll squirm and say something like, *"Wait! I never said that I'm ready to buy this! Why don't you leave some information, and I can get back to you after I've had a chance to think it over, talk to my spouse, talk to my partners, etc.?"*

Then you have to go into objection handling mode. These old sales gurus teach you how to assume the sale, then they teach you how to handle objections and resistance that they themselves cause by the way they teach you how to sell! Yikes, facepalm!

Sales Myth #6: Always Be Closing—the ABCs of Closing the Sale

How about DEF? As in Don't Ever Follow this antiquated sales myth. In fact, we should really be following the ABDs of Closing—Always Be Disarming!

Here are the different kinds of closings, none of which work with the New Model of establishing trust.

> **Optional close:** *"Do you want the red one or the blue one?"*
>
> **Invitational close:** *"Why don't you give it a try?"*
>
> **Assumptive close:** *"OK, I'll go ahead and schedule this. Do you want to take delivery Tuesday afternoon or Wednesday morning?"*
>
> **Choice close:** *"Are we doing the contract in your name or your company's name?"*
>
> **Demonstrative close:** *"If I could show you the very best investment you could ever make, would you want to see that?"*

When you use the words, *"If I could show you?"* who does the focus fall on? It focuses on you. So you've now put yourself in a position to have to prove that your product/service is the best available. We know that trust is dead in the post-trust era, so when you set yourself up to prove something, the prospect, who is a skeptic, will try to prove you wrong. They love proving you wrong.

Instead, don't even give them a chance. Simply change the wording to *"If there was . . . ";* for instance, *"If there was an investment that could get you the returns you are looking for, would that be of interest to you?"*

By being neutral, there is no pressure to prove anything to your prospect. This removes the pressure from you, and it allows you to be relaxed. The very best sales-people are *always* neutral. Average salespeople are always one-sided because they focus on themselves rather than on their potential customers and their customers' problems. Remember, neutral environments in sales are safe and relaxed environments, and most sales happen in a relaxed atmosphere, as Jeffrey Gitomer says.

While traditional closing questions may sound good, today's consumers, for the most part, don't fall for these anymore because they've heard them for decades. In today's economy, customers can use the power of technology to examine other choices from your competitors.

Today's consumer will *not* be manipulated. Today's customer doesn't want to be talked at and sold to; they want to be asked, heard, and understood.

These old sales techniques automatically cause sales resistance and pressure. Using them is what keeps you from earning the income you deserve. Like a rock star who insists on a certain brand of guitar, the New Model Salesperson would *never* use these cacophonous, lame-sounding techniques because they know it would make them average in selling and cause their audience to leave before the encore.

Now that we've cleared that up, let's take a quick look at the five key principles of the New Model of Selling.

1. The purpose of you being in sales is to find and help other people solve their problems. During the engagement process, you'll ask questions to discover problems, find out what caused those problems, and understand how they've affected your prospects' lives. You've got to be a problem finder, and one that's laser-focused on helping your prospects solve their problems. That means detaching yourself from making a sale and instead, focusing on whether or not there's a sale to be made in the first place.

2. Timing is everything, especially when it comes to asking the right questions at the right time, but not questions that are designed to get people to say what you want them to say. You'll need to toss out highly skilled questions that bring out people's inner and external truths, and most importantly, all the feels, as in their emotions.

3. Listen up and listen closely to what your prospect means, not just what they say. This includes letting go of waiting for an opportunity to speak or thinking about what you're going to say next. It means slowing down, not assuming anything, and listening to what is *behind* their problems,

without any of your personal interpretations or judgments intervening. It means being completely open.

4. Using the commitment formula to close means summarizing the prospect's main problems and the emotional pain caused by them, and then, briefly describing what it is you do, making sure to include the benefits of the features you have that will satisfy the emotional problem they're dealing with. Next steps of this formula are asking a qualifying question and then asking them to clarify their answer by asking why. Last, but not least, you toss out a committing question to help them close themselves.

5. Eliminate sales pressure and resistance by building trust, using neutral language, and even more importantly, focusing on the prospect and what they're looking for, not on your own agenda of making a sale.

All five principles can play Six Degrees of Kevin Bacon, and in this case, the Kevin Bacon is neuro-emotional persuasion questions (NEPQ) because, when you use these questions, you find out fast whether there is a sale to be made, you build trust, and you allow prospects to persuade themselves. And you take the stress, the pressure, and the resistance out of the sales equation. It's like all of Kevin Bacon's best movies—*Footloose, Diner, Apollo 13, A Few Good Men*, and, debatably, *Wild Things*, all in one.

Now you're ready to cut loose and delve deeper into each stage of the NEPQ-infused New Model sales process. Let's start with finding out how to verbally maneuver our way past the gatekeeper, shall we?

Chapter 3

Unlocking the Gatekeeper

I only have three things to do. I have to choose the right people,
allocate the right number of dollars, and transmit ideas from one
division to another with the speed of light. So I'm really in the
business of being the gatekeeper and the transmitter of ideas.
—Jack Welch

If you've ever been to a party or a nightclub, you've seen the velvet ropes, and you may have even had them parted for you like Charlton Heston did to the Red Sea in *The Ten Commandments* or like Steve Rubell did for Liza and Halston at Studio 54. The doorkeeper was the decider of your social fate that night. Did you get in or go home and sulk about your social failure into a can of White Claw? In sales, we face similar challenges.

Getting past the gatekeeper is among the most common challenges sales-people face, and in the modern world, you will encounter many. The ability to get through what some may view as a potential roadblock is a critical skill for earning time with new prospects. Still, many salespeople lack a strategic approach to engaging with gatekeepers successfully. Because if you don't get past the gate-keeper, nothing else happens, and unlike that VIP section you couldn't get into, this is your livelihood and not just a big night out.

"Treat everyone you meet as though they're the most important person you'll meet today," wrote Roger Dawson, author, and founder of the Power Negotiation Institute and, according to *SUCCESS* magazine, "America's premier business negotiator." And while Dawson's 100 percent spot on, successful salespeople today treat the gatekeepers *even better* than that because it's those people who hold the access code removing that firewall to their success.

In some companies (large or small), there is a receptionist sitting at a desk that you will definitely want to build a very friendly relationship with (often in major companies there are two or three people who play that role). It is crucial that if you will be going there with any degree of frequency, you need to get to know them. As Jerry always notes, treat them like they are important because they are. They often have information about who controls access to the person you want to see or who is allowed in or out. You also do not know who they know at that big company so being seen positively by them is a great idea. Far too many salespeople pay them little to no attention. Everyone has an invisible tattoo that says, "Make me feel important." Building a relationship with them makes them feel as important as they are!

Once they give you the green light to go see the "real" gatekeeper and you get upstairs, then the same concepts apply. Treat them like the truly important person they are. If you have developed that relationship as we have in many large companies, the conversation will be natural and likely fun. Should you be there for the very first time, then be prepared to ask for access to the decision maker, but *only* after you have attempted to develop a relationship with that gatekeeper. Ask them questions like

"Do you mind telling me a little about yourself?"
"How long have you been with the company?"
"Can you help me get a feel for how long she ordinarily likes to spend with visitors like me?"

Remember, you would not be "upstairs" if it weren't 98 percent likely that the prospect or customer is going to see you. Focus on building the relationship.

If they ask you *"What do you do?"* your answer could be similar to the following:

"You know how some of your patients with a broken leg can have a hard time being compliant with their boot because they are anxious to progress, and their impatience might wind up worsening their fracture?

"We launched this product three months ago and the physicians that have learned about it are very excited about how this technology can help avoid additional trauma to the broken bone due to noncompliance. What we do is provide a small chip that will fit in any boot that can alert your office if indeed someone might be in danger of a setback with that broken leg because they stop wearing the boot. Do you think this new technology might be something that Dr. Smith would want to know more about?"

It is important to always be looking *and* listening for common ground and any potential opportunities to show your thoughtfulness after you leave. For example, if they (the gatekeeper) say they have a twenty-one-year-old daughter who is unsure of what she wants to do when she graduates in the spring, then maybe you respond this way:

"I know it's an exciting time for her and your whole family. Can I suggest an easy book to read that she might like and it could help her make up her mind? It's called Risk Forward *by Victoria Labalme, and it was written for the large number of people everywhere who are unsure of what to do next. It's a fast and fun read, and it may help her move forward faster after she graduates. Check it out and let me know what you think next time we touch base, OK?"*

Also, before you leave, be sure to ask

"It was great meeting with you and getting to know you. What's usually the best way for me to reach you if I have a question that I'm sure you can probably help me with, and I sure don't want to be seen as a pest by anyone in your office?"

Lastly, make sure they have your contact information and have a quick understanding of why they might want to reach out to you.

Valerie Sokolosky, one of the founding experts and authors instrumental in propelling the image consulting and business etiquette industries, says that to win over the gatekeeper and have them part those proverbial velvet ropes, you have to treat them as clients and appeal to their emotions too. "If you don't have the person's heart, she won't want to keep listening to you. If you are just another number, no matter who you are or what you say, there is nothing you can do," she says. "You can do everything right, and there is a wall. And if you can't break it down, you can't break it down." And, unlike today's newspapers and magazines, there's no paywall. You either break it down or you don't.

Once you get your gatekeeper groove on, you'll realize it's not that hard to break down that wall. By building a relationship with the gatekeeper, you'll improve your odds of success. No one likes a name-dropper. When it comes to the gatekeeper, being on a first-name basis with him or her isn't just money, it's priceless.

The gatekeeper's role is often played by a company's receptionist or a decision maker's administrative assistant. They are put in place to help by answering the phone (ahem, screening calls) and turning away those they think are unimportant. Many gatekeepers develop a level of frustration toward outsiders. This is understandable if you consider that salespeople have been known to frequently resort to manipulation to get past them to reach the decision maker. A gatekeeper who allows the wrong person access to the boss will likely be reprimanded, so they're motivated to do their job well.

While often glossed over, gatekeepers are often some of the most intelligent, intuitive, and essential staffers, and as such, you'll need to adopt a specific mindset to influence them. Unlike that pesky paywall, they can't be bought. The former models of selling may tell you to avoid the gatekeeper or go directly above them. Great idea—if pissing them off is your goal.

They're not called gatekeepers because it sounds like a character out of a dystopian sci-fi flick. These people are great assets to your prospects' business. Treat them as such. As Albert Einstein once said, "I speak to everyone in the same way, whether he is the garbage man or the president of the university." And remember, gatekeepers are well versed in sales schtick, so you have to shake things up a bit to stand out.

First, let go of your attachment to making the sale and focus on whether there is a sale to be made in the first place. To succeed, you need to be detached from the expectations of making a sale. In this example, let's say you had the direct line of the decision maker, but when you called, they didn't answer. So why not call into the main line and ask the receptionist or gatekeeper to find out where they are?

> **New Model Salesperson:** *"Hi, I'm wondering whether you could help me out for a second? I am trying to get a hold of Alex and I got his voice mail. Would you happen to know if he's in a meeting, possibly at lunch, or even on vacation by* any *chance?"*

Notice that you are not just asking the gatekeeper to find Alex. You're also offering possible solutions to finding Alex. There is zero sales pressure placed on the receptionist; this is just a normal conversation.

The gatekeeper is usually going to give you one of three answers:

1. He's in a meeting.
2. He's at lunch right now.
3. He's out of town/on vacation/on a business trip.

Their answer will give you more information than you'd get if you had just left a voice mail. Now you know where your prospect is so you can call back at a more appropriate time either that day or when you know they will be back to have a "live" conversation.

But wait! The receptionist could also say, *"No, I don't know where Alex is today."* In this case, don't push, just reply with a very low-key statement such as, *"That's not a problem."* This type of *relaxed* statement will diffuse any sales pressure the receptionist might be feeling.

You then can say, *"By any chance, would you happen to know anyone close to his desk or office who works in his area that would know where he is or when he would be available?"*

Here, you are just offering another option for the receptionist. Many times, they will say yes and transfer you to someone in the office who would know where Alex is.

In *The Best Story Wins: How to Leverage Hollywood Storytelling in Business and Beyond*, Pixar and *The Simpsons* writer Matthew Luhn describes the battleground of modern sales. He says, "You have eight seconds to convince people that you've got something worth hearing about before they zone out, tune out, or check out." Eight seconds! Fans of the musical *Rent* know that a year is composed of 525,600 minutes, but to put the eight seconds into perspective, let's consider things that happen in such a fleeting time span.

A well-choreographed IndyCar pit stop takes eight seconds, and we're sure there are several TikTok challenges people can do in eight seconds or less. *8 Seconds* was also the title of a B-list 1994 Western flick starring Luke Perry and Stephen Baldwin and was named for the length of time a bull rider is required to stay on for a ride to be scored. Obscure, yes, but in other words, there aren't many things one can do in that short amount of time, and we're tasking you here with convincing someone to listen to you. Not easy, but completely doable.

Personalized Introduction

Remember, you've only got eight seconds to stay on that bull or change that tire—or even less to get the gatekeeper's attention! That's why it's crucial to create a personalized introduction to help you stand out. Doing this enables you to tell people concisely and efficiently what you do and how it helps other people. This is also a one-size-fits-all for prospects.

Take this scenario: A salesperson calls a doctor's office to talk to a lead. A gatekeeper answers. Here is what the Average Salesperson who still uses traditional sales techniques would say:

> **Gatekeeper:** *"Well, what do you do?"*
> **Average Salesperson:** *"I am with XYZ Company, and we are a world-leading pharmaceutical company with this new medication called XYZ Medication that really will help your patients with their blood pressure. Physicians all over the world are just raving about it. In fact, we have been rated the number one solution by doctors in your state the last three years in a row . . ."*

Then what happens? As you may have experienced, the prospect or the gate-keeper is going to say something like, *"We already use someone for that,"* *"We don't need that,"* *"We're not interested,"* or *"Can you call me back in a week [a month, a year . . .]?"* and, after all that, you make no sale?!

The top 1 percent of salespeople know that to attract potential customers like a magnet, they don't have to tell people *what* they do but *how* what they do helps other people. The response focuses on general challenges that most people can identify with and are aware of. This demonstrates the *purpose* to help other people solve these problems.

Let's look at another example. Say the New Model Salesperson sells financial services to high-net-worth investors or institutions.

> **Prospect:** *"What do you do?"*
>
> **New Model Salesperson:** *"Well, you know how a lot of high-net-worth inves-tors are sometimes concerned with their investments because of the volatility in the market, up and down economic growth, and the central banking policy? What we do is we have a proprietary investment blend that has a twenty-year track record of paying our investors very substantial returns. And, at the same time, because of our unique financial structure, we are able to do that with minimal risk."*

Do you think investors are concerned with the volatility of the market? Do you think they want to protect their principal investments? Uh, again, is water wet? Hello!

Here is an example of what I (Jeremy) would say if someone asked me what I do:

> *"Well, you know how a lot of companies sometimes get frustrated by losing sales to low-cost competitors? They're concerned about their sales teams incon-sistently hitting sales targets and are just really worried about the lack of results from their salespeople. What we do is we help companies like that by training their teams on how to sell using specific questions and techniques that work with human behavior, so they are viewed as the* trusted author-

ity in the market, which allows them to charge more and be able to hit their sales targets at the same time."

Then you ask a question at the end of your personalized intro, such as, *"What do you guys do to train your salespeople?"*

Now it's your turn to build your own personalized introduction. A great personalized introduction includes three parts:

- Problem
- Solution
- Question

Let's look at each one of these.

The Problem

Start your reply with the phrase *"You know how . . . "* and add two to three of the biggest generic problems with which your prospects would identify. Of course, these need to be problems that your solution will actually solve and not something Seinfeld would ask at the beginning of his show, although that could be fun, too, but never mind. Repeat: eight seconds, eight seconds.

The New Model Salesperson is a sales therapist of sorts, serving as a problem finder and a problem solver, not a product pusher. Your job is to discover their problems, find out what's causing those problems, and determine how those problems are affecting your potential customer. You got this!

The Solution

This is where you demonstrate how what you do helps people solve their challenges. The key here is to use very simple language and don't go overboard and start screaming like an As Seen on TV salesman. No "ACT NOW and get two for the price of one!" tactics. Be somewhat generic and restrained here.

Start with *"Well, what I do is help people/companies* [insert what you've deemed to be their specific problems here]*"* and continue with how your solution *solves* those problems. Make like a Ginsu knife (Google alert for our millennial and Gen

Z friends) and slice and dice your way right through it.

The Question

Here, you ask a question that turns the focus back onto the other person to explore and uncover what their problems are and whether you can help them. Let's say you sell a financial services product. Open things up by asking something like, *"I'm curious, what do you invest in yourself?"* or *"What does your portfolio look like?"*

Posing these types of questions immediately puts the focus on your prospect instead of yourself. That will help you connect with them *way* better than any traditional old method of selling ever will. Because, really, besides having to listen to the worst song ever recorded, Starship's "We Built This City," on repeat, there are few things more insufferable than a person talking about themselves on an endless loop.

Your personalized introduction is not meant to sell them; it's just meant to make them not want to put you on mute and, instead, want to engage in a two-way conversation to see whether you can help them. Selling to business-to-business (B2B) markets is much more complex than business-to-consumer (B2C). In fact, B2B can involve anywhere from six to ten decision makers, so the challenge has become more complicated than ever before. The path to purchase is not linear. Therefore, you have to go in standing out and setting yourself apart from your competitors—costumes and gimmicks not required—though you would probably go viral if you dressed up like a sales sloth.

As Harvard Business School professor Michael Porter said, "Strategy is about setting yourself apart from the competition. It's not a matter of being better at what you do—it's a matter of being different at what you do."

B2B sales also require you to build relationships like LEGO, brick by brick, because these companies are complex and layered. But more like Jenga, you'll need to figure out carefully where and how to go in without damaging the foundation. Once you're in, you still have to figure out whether you can stay, by assessing whether there is even an opportunity for you to continue to spread your branded wisdom throughout the rest of the organization by leveraging relationships.

For smaller transactional sales, quick phone outreach, social media engagement, and email blasts may be enough. Most people are familiar with transactional sales—they are the everyday, straightforward buying and selling of products and services to an individual or small group of individuals (think: magazine subscriptions, printers at Staples, cell phones, auto insurance, etc.).

For the most part, these types of transactions are low risk with a short sales cycle. Many startups focus on transactional sales early on in their business. These sales typically have a one- or two-call-close sales cycle. It's about selling single products and services (or small bundles) and is driven by marketing and sales rather than by relationships. Just think of it as casually dating versus a Facebook-official, committed relationship.

Complex sales are the serious relationships, requiring nurturing and precise knowledge of your prospects' specific needs. It, like most relationships, also requires patience. We've learned a thing or two we want to teach you about the hyper-focused, targeted outreach necessary for complex sales.

A complex sale is more high risk, and may include many stakeholders, high investment, and a longer sales cycle. It's like *Game of Thrones*, which featured seventy-three episodes broadcast over eight seasons (or, in some people's cases, just weeks of bleary-eyed binge-watching), versus *Mare of Easttown*, which featured just seven episodes in just over a month.

With higher investment comes higher risk and greater complexity. The sales rep must balance the organization's needs with the capabilities of the product or service to deliver a custom, large-scale solution. These sales take *months* to process as the client considers the proposed solutions and weighs your product/service against your competitors' product/service. Because of this added complexity, you will see better results using a different approach.

In many cases, it happens over a series of events that can take months to understand and sometimes years to get in front of. As a result, your prospects may be engaged for months before they show interest in moving forward. Aristotle wasn't kidding when he said, "Patience is bitter, but its fruit is sweet." Hang in there.

As *Game of Thrones* author George R. R. Martin sagely said, "Different roads sometimes lead to the same castle." That same castle will usually have several moats and gatekeepers, so it's never wise to overlook the gatekeeper. Results may likely be in your favor when you do the opposite. Be willing to get to know who they are. Be kind, be vested, build trust. You never know, they may have a killer recipe to spice up your Taco Tuesdays too.

Humanize Them

Viewing gatekeepers as insurmountable security guards or behemoth bouncers instead of seeing them for the people they are won't get you very far. It doesn't sell. If you want to increase your sales, you cannot dehumanize the gatekeeper, turning them into an ogre and not the lovable kind like Shrek. They take their roles seriously and want to be seen as the professionals they are, so let's treat them that way. Treat everyone as if they are important *because* they are! They can expedite access if they see you as genuine and different from pushy reps who do not treat them as an important and vital member of the team.

It's human nature for people to want to feel important or, for the humble types, at the very least, needed. The easiest way to oblige is to politely, not intrusively, take a genuine interest in them: ask them about the difficulty of their role, ask them about their family, ask them how they wound up in this part of the country, ask what they do when they aren't working. Instead of walking in or calling and asking how they are, consider speaking to them as if you don't have an agenda. Demonstrate that you care. Talk about their interests for the sake of talking about their interests. Look for common ground. Who knows, you may end up with a new interest in competitive dog grooming or extreme ironing, and if not, you will walk away with some excellent cocktail conversations.

When you do this, they will lower their guard and see you as a person too, rather than as someone to avoid like the nosy neighbor or the horrendous Tinder date. Treat them like an *influential* figure, because, frankly, they are more influential to you at this point than the one million-follower Instagram account your tween daughter follows. Make no mistakes about it, the person behind the company you want to work with thought highly enough of them to put them in that position, and you should definitely do the same.

In a world of automation, robot restaurant servers, and a hybrid approach to business, there's still a serious desire for human connection. It takes time and skills, but it's worth it for you and your prospects. People seek humanized customer experiences, which could be why all those self-checkout counters always seem to have human employees hovering around them, or it could just be that they're better at checking us out than we are, but you get it. One of the most requested improvements in sales is better human interaction.

The need for more empathetic, personalized service also translates to the sales process. As a McKinsey study found, 70 percent of purchasing experiences are based on how the customer feels they are being treated.[4] Such statistics show that customers want to be valued and treated as individuals and not as numbers or quotas.

Learn Who They Are

Once you let go of the pressure to push past them and mow them down like an overzealous bargain hunter in hot pursuit of a $49 flat screen on Black Friday and truly see them as people just like you, it's important to get to know who that person is. According to a 2017 Harvard study[5] published in the *Journal of Personality and Social Psychology*, asking a question, and then asking at least two follow-up questions will dramatically increase how likable you are, so ask away!

As Jerry always says, people love to talk about themselves, so get that gatekeeper talking. Ask them about their day, or their favorite sports team, movie, band, or food. You want to be on a first-name basis with the people connected to your prospects even if they admit their fave band is Nickelback. Remember, this isn't a quest to find a spouse; it's the building of a business relationship.

Aside from some research, you don't know who you are talking to when it comes to the gatekeeper. Jerry has discovered countless times over his storied career that the receptionist can be a close family friend or relative of the company vice president. The executive assistant can be the CEO's wife's cousin's best friend. You get the idea. You never know who you're talking to, but you should make it a point to figure that out ASAP with nonthreatening questions.

Build Trust

Because trust has become a unicorn of sorts in sales, gatekeepers are equally as skeptical as your prospects, if not more skeptical, so you must build trust with them too. They're the ones with the all-access, backstage pass to that coveted appointment, not to mention they're the ones with the prospect's mobile number.

Once you've pulled off the scary, Scooby-Doo villain mask and humanized the gatekeeper and or the prospect into your ally by learning about who they are, it's time to move on to the trust-building phase.

In romance, the term "engagement" refers to a period of getting to know each other before marriage (plus, traditionally, involves a diamond ring), and in communication and sales, it has a very similar meaning (minus that ring). Trust only revolves around relationships. In the post-trust era, this has become the dominating factor in your success as a salesperson.

More than ever before, we salespeople must engage our prospects as individual people, as human beings, before we can move forward with our solutions.

The way you build a relationship with people is through your actions. And your actions must be consistent, persistent, and predictable over time. Once people feel they can trust you, they'll listen to you. The first interaction with somebody in a complex sale should only have one goal. It's to get that person to talk to you again. And how do you do that? You've got to build trust. Remember to focus on *them* and *their* world, and you will remain safe in their minds as the salesperson they should go with because they trust you and your intent to help them. You're not just there to just sell them.

If you have a valuable business relationship with somebody, three things are true. The first thing is you have access when you need it. So, if you call them, they're going to call you back without any hesitation. The second thing is you can influence that person. And what that means is that person will listen to you differently. The difference between having a conversation with a stranger and someone you have built a relationship with is the relationship carries the interest. The third thing is that you're doing something to help this person succeed. In Hebrew, that's called doing a mitzvah. A good deed. Indeed.

Jerry has a fantastic story that perfectly encapsulates this method. As a pharmaceutical rep, Jerry had a physician who wouldn't see reps in his office. He was probably the biggest doctor in Alabama. One day Jerry's rep calls him and asks, "How do I get in to see Dr. McAtee?" Jerry asked, "What's your relationship with the office?" The rep told Jerry he had a great relationship with the staff, so Jerry proceeded.

"Does he stick to a routine?" Jerry questioned.

"He's very good about it," the rep confirmed. "He is at the hospital every morning at six."

"OK." Jerry paused. "Well, you can show up there once a week at six in the morning. Walk with him into the hospital and say something along the lines of, 'How about them Dodgers?'"

Because Jerry regularly spoke with the employees, they told him the doc was a huge Dodgers fan, and he knew he could use that information in the future. Remember to always listen to the gatekeeper and those around them. *All* information is useful.

"Three or four weeks into this," Jerry continued, "he's going to look at you and ask who you are. When he asks, you respond, 'Well, I'm actually a drug rep, and I know I can't see you in the office. I'd love to have a conversation with you, but I don't want to bother you at all or be seen by you as pushy.'"

After Jerry's rep did that, the doctor offered him a chance to sit down and go over his presentation. I was amazed by this story. That one encounter led to him landing the *biggest* prescriber in the history of that product, and it all started with the LA Dodgers and building a relationship with the gatekeeper.

The best advice for getting past the gatekeeper is that you need to stop sounding like everyone else. You must humanize the sales conversation early in the relationship by making them feel as important as they truly are because you need their help to learn about the customer or prospect. People love to be helpful *if* they think you are genuine and not a "slick salesperson." Spoiler alert: those are exactly the types they are paid to keep out.

Once you do that, they'll feel that you are authentic about your intentions. You aren't like other salespeople. You truly want to see whether you can help them. But you can't go into it like they do on *American Ninja Warriors*. You have to go in less aggressively and more strategically. Little by little, your customer will reveal themselves, but if you go at it too fast, they'll pull away. Start with something unrelated to sales—something you know they are into. This is how you'll create trust and differentiate yourself from your competitors at the same time.

But first, let's tackle those dreaded cold calls. In this era of text messaging, one would think that cold calls are the appendix of the sales biz, a vestigial organ of the olden days. But, alas, they're not. They're still very useful and don't all have to be dreaded like a trip to the dentist.

Cold Calls That Don't Trigger Sales Resistance

An *Inc.* magazine article titled "Why People Don't Make Phone Calls Anymore, According to Psychology"[6] said what we already know: "Increasingly, people are shunning the phone in favor of chat apps and texting, not just in the workplace, but as consumers." And, we're not saying that cold calls never work, because Jerry has an acquaintance with a $15 million biz based entirely on cold calls, but it's a crapshoot these days. Still, cold calls have yet to go the way of the beeper, and salespeople are still making them.

How many other calls from salespeople do you think your potential customers get on a weekly or daily basis? Salespeople call them every single day to pitch their products or services. They all claim that their products/services are the best. Therefore, potential customers have become overly sensitive when the phone rings and it's someone they don't know. Your potential customers are automatically skeptical about the salesperson who's calling them. Your prospects have all gotten very good at reading the subtle and not-so-subtle signals that come from our words and tone of voice—that is, if they even take the call in the first place.

This is how prospects can feel if the caller is just some random salesperson who is trying to sell them something. Your goal is not to sound like every other salesperson who calls them every. single. day.

OK, so the phone rings. They don't hit decline and they answer your call. What usually happens in a matter of seconds? Before you have said anything past your usual opener of *"Hello, my name is X, I'm with ABC Company, and what we do is . . . ,"* it's pretty much over, isn't it?

Why do cold calls break down in a matter of seconds? Well, 99 percent of salespeople start out with a "predictable" sales pitch while they close their eyes and keep talking, in hopes the other person stays on the line to listen, right?

What do you think is going on in the person's mind when you are doing your sales pitch? If eye rolls could talk, right? What goes on in your mind when a salesperson cold calls you and proceeds to do a sales pitch?

Maybe you get defensive and look for ways to get rid of the salesperson who's calling you, correct? Or, gasp, you just hang up. You're breaking up, bad connection, right? Cold calls break down most of the time for the simple fact that your prospect feels that you are trying to sell them something. Why?

Because the momentum we are trying to impose triggers sales resistance and self-defense mechanisms that our prospects use to protect themselves from what they feel is an intrusion. Prospects reject salespeople when they feel sales pressure from someone who doesn't know anything about their world and just wants to force feed their solution down their throat.

Let's see how a salesperson using traditional selling techniques makes a cold call to a lead selling digital services using both old-school and New Model methods.

> **Average Salesperson:** *"Hi, is this John? John, my name is Phineas T. Barnum, and I am from XYZ Company, and the reason why I called you today was . . ."* [Starts talking about his/her solution, and hopes and prays something they say will magically trigger the prospect to want to listen to them.]
>
> **Prospect:** *"We already have that service, so we wouldn't be interested."*
>
> **Average Salesperson:** *"Well I know that we can save you more time and money by switching to our company. Can I just have two minutes of your time to go over this with you and show you what the XYZ service can do for you?"*
>
> **Prospect:** *"Look, I'm just too busy right now. If you call me next week, then maybe I can hear you out."* [Spoiler Alert: the prospect says this just to get rid of the salesperson.]
>
> **Average Salesperson:** *"Great, OK, I will call you next week and go over this with you. I know you will love what we do, and I know we can save you time and money."*

Now, what just happened here? Do you really think the prospect answered the phone a week later when the salesperson called? Uh, is water dry?

Let's take a look at this call for a moment.

Most salespeople have been taught to say the same, predictable opening. It's so predictable that you can almost lip sync it like the lead singer of an uber-popular boy band: *"Hi my name is Dustin Timberpond. I'm from XYZ Company, and the reason why I called you today is . . ."* Yawn. You may as well say bye, bye, bye before you even say hello.

Or how about this one:

"Hi, my name is Josephine Fatone. I'm from the XYZ Company and what we do is . . ."

And then what usually happens within seven to ten seconds? Yup, you got it. The greatest hits of NO. "Not interested," "We already have that," "I'm too busy to talk right now," or "We don't have any money for that." What results is a litany of objections triggered by how the salesperson started the call. Said salesperson never had a chance. It was game over at hello. Oof.

Now let's take a look at how the New Model Salesperson would start off the cold call.

> **New Model Salesperson:** *"Hello, is Larry Styles there?*
>
> **Prospect:** *"Yeah, this is Larry."*
>
> **New Model Salesperson:** *Hey Larry, this is just Justin Scott. I was wondering if you could possibly help me out for a moment?"*
>
> **Prospect:** *"Sure, how can I help you?"*
>
> **New Model Salesperson:** *"I'm not quite sure you're the person I should be talking to, but I called your office to see if your company would be opposed to looking at any possible hidden gaps or issues around your offline market-ing that you're doing or have done in the past, that could be causing you to overspend on your ads each month?"*
>
> **Prospect:** *"Who's this? What's this all about?"*
>
> **New Model Salesperson:** *"Oh I apologize, I didn't mean to offend you, What we do is, you know how . . ."* [And then you're going to go over your personalized intro on how what you do helps other people.]

Let's say the prospect replies, *"We already have an agency."* That's OK, it's not game over.

You can then reply with something like, *"Yeah, that's pretty normal, and to be frank, I am not sure we can even help you yet. I would have to know a little bit more about what you are doing with your offline advertising and how that looks to see whether we can even help you. And if we can't, we can just end the call, or I might be able to suggest someone to you who could better help you in that area. Would that be appropriate?"*

Whether you can help them or not, you are establishing yourself as a problem finder and problem solver here, and that is likely to open some doors.

When the individual has no idea who you are and no idea what the problem or your solution is, they're the coldest of cold prospects. They don't even know they have a problem. Because they are completely unaware, they think everything is fine in their business right now; your solution is not on their radar. However, when you disarm the prospect where they want to engage with you and open up to you, then you start to peel back the layers to expose the severity of their problems.

So right after our problem statement, most of the time they will ask, *"Now, who are you?"* or *"What is this all about?"* and you will simply go right into how what you do helps other people.

Here is an example: let's say you sell lead services or advertising. Here's how a New Model Salesperson does it right, with a relaxed, conversational tone. Also listen for the neutral language used:

> **New Model Salesperson:** *"You know how a lot of businesses nowadays are sometimes finding it harder to advertise with the increasing cost of ads, too many competitors, and all the changes in advertising going on all the time? Well, what we do is help companies like that target higher quality leads at a lower ad cost so they can start keeping more of their money rather than wasting it on ad campaigns that just don't work."*

Right after your personalized intro, you always want to ask a question such as this:

> *"Does that resonate with you or is it something your company might/could be experiencing?"*

Or if you feel the prospect is really into what you just said, you could skip that question and go right into your first situation question such as this:

> *"Now I guess I should probably ask what you guys do for advertising now to generate leads just to see if I could actually help you?"*

This is an essential New Model question that rests on our core principle: salespeople are the most persuasive when they allow the customer to persuade themselves.

Here is another version that can be used after the problem statement and personalized introduction:

> *"Before I go through who we are, what we do, and all that kind of boring stuff, it might be appropriate if we knew a little bit more about your company and what you do for advertising now to see whether we could actually even help you. For example, what forms of advertising do you use now to generate leads?"*

Let's say they get snippy after that question and reply with a curt, *"What are you selling?"* You can then reply with:

> *"Oh, I apologize if I have offended you. I'm not actually convinced that I could even help you yet. And it might be appropriate if we asked each other a few questions to see whether what we do could even help you. Would that work? [or] Would that be appropriate?"*

Most will say *"Sure"* or *"Yeah, that's fine."* Then it's time to take a deep dive into your situation questions. By apologizing, you are diffusing any sales tension that your potential customer may feel. Since most of your prospects receive calls every day from salespeople who use the traditional selling techniques, they may instinctively respond in a defensive, posturing way.

You may occasionally get a prospect who may be downright disrespectful and rude toward you, and at that point, it would be entirely appropriate for you to disengage from that conversation completely.

You have been authentic, warm, and most importantly, human in the conversation, but if your prospect cannot connect with that, then there is absolutely nothing you can do to help that person besides send them a book on etiquette or anger management. You *can* say, *"I'm sorry I couldn't help you,"* and then hang up and move on to someone you can help and who is willing to allow you to do so.

Notice the difference between the two approaches. The traditional selling approach focuses on you as a salesperson, but the New Model focuses on the prospect, their problems, the cause of their problems, and how said problems are affecting them.

Which approach do you think makes the potential customer feel more relaxed and comfortable: the traditional method of pitching your solution right off the bat or the New Model of Selling that focuses on your potential customer and their problems? New Model Salesperson to Traditional Salesperson: "Hold my beer."

You will know whether you are connecting with them and having an effective conversation based on how much of their history they share with you. The more skilled the questions you ask them are, they more they will open up to you.

By listening and asking highly skilled questions, your prospects will tell you things they have never told a salesperson before (hopefully business-related, of course, though be prepared for a life story because those sometimes slip in when the person really trusts you). You'll learn facts and feelings about their situation and problems and what those problems are doing to them and/or their company.

Then, you'll arrive at one of three destination points with your prospect:

Destination 1: They have no need.

Destination 2: They have a need but no real desire to change their situation.

Destination 3: They have a need and a real desire to change their situation.

Obviously, we're all rooting for what's behind Destination 3, but you'll get to one of these destinations based on the answers you receive to your questions. Remember, the answers you receive from your customers are your GPS navigation directions. Just follow them to get to your destination, a.k.a. the sale. Don't veer off course—the answers they give you when you ask clarifying, under-the-surface questions relating to what they have already told you are the key to your timely arrival at a conclusion as to whether or not this is going to lead to a sale.

When you have a complete understanding of your potential customer, you'll make more appointments, get more commitments, and make more sales faster and easier than anything else you have ever done.

As executive speech coach Patricia Fripp so fabulously said, "It is not your customer's job to remember you. It is your obligation and responsibility to make sure they don't have the chance to forget you."

Referrals

If you don't ask, you don't get, so if some of those cold calls seem to be freezing up, ask for a referral. As you start to implement the New Model, you'll eventually do less and less cold calling, and you'll have a higher percentage of referrals instead. Referrals are so much easier to sell to than a random stranger if you have the right questions in your arsenal.

Here's how to start the conversation.

> **New Model Salesperson:** *"I appreciate the opportunity to be able to help you. Can I ask you, in your mind, how do you feel I've been able to help you the most?"*

Why do we ask this? Because they're going to tell themselves how you have helped them . . . and when they do that, they own it.

> **New Model Salesperson:** *"With that in mind, who do you know that might be struggling with . . . ?"*

And then—boom, plug in the problem you just solved for them. An example might look like this. Let's say you sell merchant processing:

> *"With that in mind, who do you know that might be struggling with overpaying for merchant processing?"*

Once they've suggested a friend or business associate, the New Model Salesperson then asks for more information. Note the way in which this is asked—or, more specifically, the tone.

> **New Model Salesperson:** *"Can you please tell me a little bit more about this person and why you feel I could help them?"*

Why do you want them to tell you more? It goes back to finding out more about the person before you call, but we also want the person to own this. That way, they're more likely to contact this person and talk you up.

> **New Model Salesperson:** *"Well, how do you think it would be best to approach them? Do you feel like you should communicate to him first that I will be calling?"*

Why would we want to ask this question? Because we want the person referring them to reach out to them first. It's more powerful that way. When someone says, *"I'm sending you somebody that I think might be able to help you,"* you're more likely to get hold of them and convert them to a potential customer.

> **New Model Salesperson:** *"What do you think you should say?"*

Though this seems a little intrusive, think about why you may want to know what they're going to say to that person. For one, you want to be able to prevent them from saying anything that could create resistance with that person—anything too technical, or inaccurate, or downright weird. It's key that you set this up right. So offer a suggestion to help communicate the right thing with the right words.

> **New Model Salesperson:** *"Can I suggest something to you? What if you talked about some of the challenges you had and that he's having right now, and how we've been able to solve those? Would that be more helpful to him?"*

In most cases, they're going to think this is a great idea.

> **New Model Salesperson:** *"So besides X, is there anyone else you feel I could help?"*

What's important for you to notice about this statement is the use of the words "you feel I could help." First, you've made it about them and how they feel, and second, people are more likely to give you referrals if you're in it to help people.

OK, so you've scored your first referral. Now let's go over how to make that first phone call.

First, let's take a quick look at what most salespeople would say when calling a referral.

Average Salesperson: *"Hey Mary, I'm John Smith with XYZ Company, and Amy asked me to give you a call and said that you'd be interested in my company's services. She said you're wanting to take your business to the next level. Do you have two minutes to talk right now about how my company can get you the results you're looking for?"*

Notice who this question was focused on—yup, the salesperson and their solution, not on the prospect. That was the first mistake. The second mistake was assuming that just because you got the referral it means they will automatically be interested. Not so fast. This salesperson has just set themselves up for an epic fail.

But it gets worse. Look:

Prospect: *"Ya, I guess this is a good time."*

Average Salesperson: *"OK great, I know you're gonna be excited about what my company can offer you today. You see, here at XYZ Company, we've been in business for ten years, and we've helped over four thousand businesses have success. Now let me tell you a few things we can do to help you get where you want to go, and then you can make an informed decision at the end about working with us."*

When you try using a *closing technique* right from the start, and you tell them what you can do along with a sales pitch and say that they can then make an *informed decision*, this person is going to feel suffocated. The pressure is mounting, and they want out.

If you're still using the phrase "informed decision," shred it. Lose it. Burn it. Toss it. Donate it to a word bank. It simply does *not* work anymore. Why do salespeople keep using this technique? It's like trying to find the gas tank on a Tesla.

Now look at how the New Model Salesperson slays the referral:

New Model Salesperson: *"Hi, is this John? This is just Jeremy Miner. A mutual friend/business associate of yours, Amy, suggested I call you, as I recently helped her with X that was causing them to Y, and she mentioned*

*to me that you might be experiencing the same challenges with that. Is this
an appropriate time to talk?"*

Notice that here, the salesperson is focused on *solving problems*. That's the
absolute best way to call.

Now, what do you do if the referral wants to meet you? Here's how to start
that conversation:

> **New Model Salesperson:** *"John it's nice to meet you, and let's do this. Just so
> I don't go over things you have already talked about with Amy, perhaps you
> can give me* **your thoughts** *on what you have discussed with her and then*
> **what you'd like to cover** *so that we could* **focus on you** *and what you*
> **might** *be looking for?"*

Boom! The New Model Salesperson just evoked the mighty *might*, an exqui-
sitely neutral word that's oh so powerful.

Leaving Voice Mail

Yes, we know most people have left voice mail for so long that their mailboxes are
full and messages date back to the days when there was only one Kardashian, but
sometimes you do have to leave them, and people actually listen to them. Most
salespeople who still use the old model of selling look at leaving a voice mail as a
dead end. However, if done properly, effective voice mails can set you apart from
any other salesperson in your industry.

Because of traditional selling techniques, most salespeople dread reaching
their prospect on the phone as much as they dread being challenged by the receptionist. As a result, salespeople tend to leave a voice mail so that they can move on
to the next prospect on their list.

We leave voice mails because we want to *avoid* the feeling of being *rejected*.
By not going back to the receptionist, we avoid being challenged and rejected by
them. Most salespeople play the numbers game. They make a lot of calls to make
themselves feel that they've worked hard.

Remember, we are only focused on whether there is a sale to be made in the first place; we are not focused solely on making the sale. We must be detached from the expectations of making a sale.

But what if you left a voice mail that got someone's attention enough to actually—gasp—call you back?! Not a traditional voice mail in which you droned on with a mini sales pitch that gets deleted halfway through, but something like this:

> *"Hi Alex, this is just Stefanie Smith... I was wondering whether you could help me out for a moment? I'm not sure whether you're the right person or not, but I am trying to reach the person who's responsible for looking after* (mention your compelling problem statement) *to see whether any department in your company might be losing revenue due to vendors overcharging you.*
> *"If that resonates with you or if that's something your company could be experiencing, you are welcome to call me back. My number is 573-578-9872, and I should be available here for a little while today if you'd like to reach me."*

Or:

> *"Hi, Mr. Lohman, this is Stefanie Smith here. I'm not quite sure if you're who I should be talking to. I called to see whether your company would be open to looking at any possible hidden gaps in your offline marketing that you might be doing or have done that could be causing you to overspend on your advertising each month.*
> *"Now if that's a problem your company might be having, you can call me back at 573-578-9872. I'll be available here for a little bit.*
> *"When we connect, I'll probably have a couple of questions about your current advertising. For instance, how you're generating leads, just to make sure we can help you in the first place.*
> *"It is possible we might not be able to help you. And if that's the case, we can just save time and end the call. Or I might be able to refer you to someone else who may have a better handle on your situation to help you. Again, my number here is 573-578-9872, and I should be available here for a bit. Talk then!"*

Voice mail like this works. Why? Because the wording creates urgency, shows you have other options, and that you're busy, not just waiting all day for their call.

Here's another scenario. Say you sell franchise opportunities, and you have a website that people respond to and leave their name, email, and phone number for you to call them back. Here is how this will go down. In a very relaxed tone, you would say:

> *"Hi Mary, you responded to our online ad two hours ago on one of our websites about possibly starting your own franchise. You would have seen our logo for XYZ Company on the site, and I was calling you back to see whether we could possibly help you. My phone number is 573-578-9872. I should be available here for a little bit today if you'd like to reach me. Talk then."*

Let's dissect this voice mail. Be as specific as possible to remind them that they responded to your ad looking for whatever your offer is because they have probably also responded to several other ads the same day they responded to yours.

They may be busy and distracted, and they may have completely forgotten that they responded to your ad, especially if they responded more than a day ago. Keep in mind that they are probably getting calls from others trying to sell them something, so they'll automatically have their guard up when they answer your call, even if they are really interested in what you sell.

Reference exactly what they responded about. In this case, you sell franchises, so you're going to reference that they responded about "possibly" starting their own franchise. Using the word "possibly" diffuses any sales pressure in the call.

Now that we've successfully gotten past the gatekeeper, cue the victory music, but don't celebrate just yet. It's now time to get customer-focused.

Chapter 4

Getting Customer-Focused

People don't buy stock. They buy people they can trust,
or people they believe they can.
—Abe Karatz, *Tucker: The Man and His Dream*

Theres's no dancing around it. People find many sales folk to be a few notches above gas station sushi. The most common words associated with them include pushy, slick, manipulative, cheat, slimy, and sleazy. Yikes, rough crowd. The notion of your typical salesperson makes many consumers feel a bit disgusted. Why? Most of it has to do with their experiences with ineffective salespeople and, of course, with the way salespeople communicate (or think we have to communicate). The traditional selling techniques cause today's consumers to run the other way when used on them. Sales resistance is usually met quicker than Secretariat ran the 1973 Kentucky Derby (one minute, fifty-nine seconds).

A survey by *HubSpot Research* found that "only a mere 3% of people consider salespeople to be trustworthy."[7] Ouch. It's depressing to be the Sunoco Sashimi Special of the business world, and we as salespeople need to look within to fix it.

Why are you a salesperson? What is your purpose in sales? Why did you choose this profession? Is it the money? The flexibility? Your knack for yapping? Sure, you have to look out for number one, but if you're solely focused on yourselves, you're just not gonna hack it. If you're customer-focused, you're not in business or sales for you; you're in business for other people.

Have you ever gone speed dating? They sit you down in a room with a ton of tables, and you have a short time to make an impression before you move on to the next person. Kind of like a used car auction, only the used car in this case is you and you're trying to come off as the Rolls Royce in a lot of lemons. Selling is a lot like speed dating. You don't have years to build a relationship. A lot of times, this conception of you is created within seconds, and if you don't do it right, you'll just come off as another piece of citrus fruit.

Let's say you were trying to get someone interested in dating you, and all you did was talk about yourself and about what you have to offer them, only focusing on you and your agenda of getting them to say yes without listening to a word they have to say or, at the very least, getting to know them, what do you think would happen? Netflix and chill, party of one, is what would happen.

We've witnessed it happen all too many times, and, unlike a box office bomb of epic proportion like the JLo/Ben Affleck disaster *Gigli*, we couldn't turn it off. It just had to play out. These improperly trained salespeople can't shake the horrible first impression they made because it's already etched into their potential prospects' minds. These sales bombs focus solely on themselves rather than on the client, who has pretty much already canceled you in their mind.

When it comes to dating and sales, your A game involves taking a step back and learning how to engage *with* people, not at them. Those with the most influence in the game are those who *study* their partner, taking the time to learn about them, show a genuine interest in them, and not be self-absorbed blowhards. You aren't here to praise yourself; save that for your workouts. You're here for your potential customers and never forget that.

The purpose of being in sales is to find and help other people solve *their* problems. Ask yourself whether your business or products can actually solve your potential clients' problems. To paraphrase JFK, ask not what your client can do for you but ask what you can do for your client.

What does the beginning of a prospect interaction look like? Do you start by talking about your company, your products, and your solutions immediately after introducing yourself like an auctioneer? I hope not. Timing is everything. If you suggest marriage on the first coffee date, you're gonna be sitting solo in that Starbucks every single time. People are going to bolt.

If you go into seller mode too early in the conversation, you're putting the attention on you rather than on the customer. And guess what happens? Absolutely nothing, that's what. You will more than likely trigger sales resistance that leads to objections quickly. Then you'll have to spend your energy refuting their objections, cartoonishly chasing after them to try and make the sale when you are the one who triggered that type of behavior from the prospect in the first place.

Your prospects have the answers you need to make a sale, you just have to ask the right questions instead of talking about how many people you helped last week or how your product is superior to your competitors'. The best way to become customer-focused is to sell based on the simplicity of this quote: "To sell Jane Brown what Jane Brown buys, you have to see the world through Jane Brown's eyes." You can't see the world through Jane Brown's eyes if you're not even trying to learn how she thinks, and no LASIK is going to cure that sales myopia. But our advice will. Read on.

If you're currently focused on what's in it for you, it's time to upgrade your operating system to focus on how you can help your prospective customers. The first thing you can do is let go of wanting to make a commission or quarterly bonus; stop placing the sale before the person. Yes, we know you need to make a living. And you will. As long as you remember it's not a numbers game! You can't treat people like they have dollar signs written on their forehead unless they literally do because, these days, you never know what sorta facial tattoos people may have. Joking aside, they are people, not money.

Be a problem finder, a problem solver, *and* focus on the prospect and helping them discover the severity of their problems to see whether what you have to offer will be beneficial or not. It is all about uncovering what's holding them back from their desires and how you can remedy that for them. Make like a sales Sherpa and guide them to achieve clarity about their current state compared to where they want to be. Help them to envision their objectives once their problems are solved by your solution. Give them their "Aha!" "Eureka!" moment!

With the New Model, engagement is now 85 percent of the sale. It's where both you and your potential customer are discovering what their problems are, what caused those problems, and how those problems are affecting them so you can see whether your solution will help them. Here is where you both get your eureka moments. If your prospect knows precisely what their problem is, whether they are hoping to buy a new computer or take a five-day cruise, they can find the information on their own to decide without you.

The services of salespeople are *far* more valuable when your prospects are mistaken, confused, or clueless about their true problems. In those situations, the ability to persuade others hinges less on problem *solving*, than on problem *finding*. This isn't *Where's Waldo?*, and finding those problems isn't nearly as difficult as you think.

Let Go of Control

Discovering and solving prospects' problems will require you to do something that very few salespeople in the world know how to do: wait for it—you have to let go of control. Can you handle it? Oh yes you can! Detach yourself from the outcome. When you let go of the outcome and use the right customer-focused approach, your sales and your income will always increase. Detach yourself from the expectations of making the sale, and instead, get customer-focused by determining whether there's a sale to be made in the first place. It all begins with having a conversation to understand a customer's perspective so we relate to them as humans and not see them as just another close.

In Jerry's book *Stop Acting like a Seller and Start Thinking like a Buyer*, he recalls a time when he was in the market for a bigger car. A loyal Infiniti customer, Jerry decided to check out BMW, where the car he was looking at there was $20,000 more than the Infiniti. When the salesman asked him a series of pointed, intuitive questions, he learned immediately that his car product wasn't for Jerry, who admitted that he only drives a car as a mode of transportation rather than for the driving experience. "Then this isn't worth the money to you, Mr. Acuff," said the salesman. "You should get the Infiniti. The Infiniti is a great car . . . the BMW is about driving a car. If you don't really love driving a car, I wouldn't spend the money if I were you."

Wait, whaaaaaaaaaaaaat? Yep, that really happened. And while Jerry did go with the Infiniti, he was so impressed by the honesty and the skilled questioning of the salesman, he admitted that the guy "laid the foundation for a future sale." Talk about establishing trust!

By detaching yourself from the outcome, you will automatically become more open to feeling and hearing your potential customers' problems and determining whether you can help them. This will also enable you to become more creative with ideas for how you can solve their problems. Let go of control, detach yourself from the sale, and position yourself as the expert. When you do this, your prospects will start to view you as a trusted authority, rather than just another smarmy salesperson trying to sell them something they don't want.

If there isn't a sale to be made, you can walk away with confidence just like that car salesman did at BMW. You can leave the conversation with peace of mind. If you truly live by the philosophies we teach, you won't have any qualms about turning business down that you don't deserve.

Great salespeople like the Beemer guy do the right thing. But how do you know it's the right thing? If you're not getting the right information out of the customer, if you're not building trust with the customer, then you don't know what the right thing is. Great salespeople facilitate the conversation to identify the issue or challenge a potential buyer is facing. When we craft and execute this conversation correctly, we create the greatest opportunity to solve their problem(s) in a meaningful way. And that way also leads to sales. So keep following it.

You're the individual who takes buyers down a path of discovery, helping them learn what their real problems are and what exactly is causing them. As the driver of a car, which you hopefully purchased with the help of a skilled salesman like the one at BMW, you can take them where you want them to go because you control what questions you ask, but they should feel like they are in control of the decision because they are.

That's an important difference there. They don't feel like you're trying to overstep your boundaries or take advantage of them. You feel like you're there to help them, which you are. You are helping them get from one destination to another. You are the sales Lyft or sales Uber, depending on which one has the better rate in rush hour. You want to challenge your prospects without degrading them. You want to challenge their way of thinking not by telling them they are wrong, but by asking questions that allow them to realize that, yup, they're actually wrong or were just thinking about it differently and got enlightened. We will go more in-depth about this later.

Do you see the difference? It's so much easier to sell when you learn how to get your prospects to chase *you* down rather than the other way around. You are helping them become more self-aware. You are doing them a solid, and sales karma will help you reap the rewards of all that goodwill.

Be Unbiased

You have strong opinions, sure. We all do. But to succeed here, you have to leave the bias at home with your comfy quarantine yoga pants. When you come from an unbiased point of view, where you're more focused on whether or not you can actually help them, people react well and open up to you because they feel your intentions are genuine.

You can eliminate bias by building a valuable business relationship where people trust you because they have witnessed your persistent, consistent, predictable actions. Or you have to use a selling approach that disarms their sales resistance because you not only know what to say but *how* to say it and how to navigate the conversation much smoother than the wobbly CGI in the Emily Blunt and Dwayne "The Rock" Johnson version of Disney's *Jungle Cruise* so they always feel in control. Anytime you're in a selling situation where the client thinks the salesperson is controlling the dialogue, your chances of success are slim.

In his book *Influence: The Psychology of Persuasion,* Robert Cialdini, Professor Emeritus of Psychology and Marketing at Arizona State University, says, "Whenever you say something negative about your product, your credibility goes up." That hasn't changed. Seeing that you are unbiased shows prospects that your honest intent is to figure out whether you can actually help them. And maybe you can't, but when they feel you are genuine, they become much more open to what you're offering, and that opening is priceless.

The buyer is always going to make the decision. Now they'll make the decision based on how much they believe in what you're saying. Jerry believes that what the prospect says is far more important than what the salesperson says. In that light, rather than spew data, he believes that when we share data, we need to follow that up and ask the customer what they think about that information and how, if at all, it might benefit their situation.

When we *tell* them what it means, they are likely to become skeptical, and they'll probably be drifting off thinking about lunch rather than the data you just spewed out *unless* you engage them by asking targeted questions.

For example, if they say, *"Well, that means it will save us money,"* that is far more powerful than us telling them that we will, indeed, save them money. The truth is, when we say it, they often doubt it. If they say it, it's true. We've seen this in action.

Someone seeking Jerry's advice went over a fifteen-minute dissertation on one of his former clients who used to buy from him. They had a contract with their competitor—a very large office with seventeen people. All of them were potential decision makers; however, the wife of the person who runs the business was the one who was making this decision.

So his question was, how do I sell these people? Before Jerry had a chance to respond, the guy said that his strategy was to go around the boss's wife and build rapport with the people with whom he had a good relationship. He asked what Jerry thought about his MO, though it was evident, by the look on Jerry's face, that he wasn't a fan.

"Let me make this clear," Jerry interjected. "You have *no* chance of convincing that person to change her mind. All you're going to do is antagonize almost everybody in that office, including the people that go to bat for you. Here's my advice. Stop calling on them. They *aren't* buying. Go find your business someplace else."

One of the biggest mistakes salespeople make, and it may be *the* biggest, is they call on the wrong people. How many times can you see the same "New phone, who dis?" response before you realize you're barking up the wrong tree? The former models make it seem as though *everyone* needs your product, and that's simply not the case. If you call on people who are never going to buy, you will never sell. If there is a sale to be made, then you continue to have the conversation.

What the New Model does is it gets the customer to say what they think, what they believe, and what they think needs to be done. And if there is synchronicity between what they're looking for and what you're offering, then you're not going to even have to sell them. They're going to buy.

Whatever you do, you cannot sound biased or preloaded with an agenda. People do not ordinarily share information freely with us if they feel or sense we are biased. They also want to feel understood, and that's why the new selling model is so powerful. These two realities of human communication are inherent in this New Model of Selling. If they wanted to purchase something from an inanimate object, they'd go to a vending machine, Amazon, or the guy at the drive-thru who never smiles no matter how hard you try to make him laugh.

Buyer's EQ

According to the *Dictionary of Psychology*, Emotional Intelligence (a.k.a. EI) is defined as "the ability to perceive, use, understand, manage, and handle emotions. People with high emotional intelligence can recognize their own emotions and those of others, use emotional information to guide thinking and behavior, discern between different feelings and label them appropriately, and adjust emotions to adapt to environments." Sounds deep, and it is. And while there's no Mensa for those with high EI, it's the key trait of most top-performing sales reps. EI and self-awareness in sales cannot be understated. In fact, when dealing with your customers, it is required.

There are telltale signs of people with low EI, and you totally know this person: they think they're always right; they're clueless about and disinterested in other people's feelings; they're insensitive, blame others for their problems, have poor coping skills, and often have emotional outbursts. If that sounds like one of your exes, well, good thing they're your exes. Low EI doesn't go very far in sales either.

As we mentioned before, the majority of purchasing decisions are not solely based on logic. The buyer and seller ultimately rely on triggers that appeal to their emotions. The more a salesperson understands the emotions invested in a sales interaction, the better their chances of successfully making the sale.

While rational factors such as pricing and features affect purchase decisions, emotions still play a large role. EI helps you be aware of your emotional state so you can control your emotions. Emotions are more than emojis. They are tools and should be used when necessary and kept in check when necessary as well. Unlike Larry David, who couldn't care less in the ironically titled *Curb Your Enthusiasm*, it's crucial that you quash your apathy, anxiety, irritation, greed, and other assorted not-so-pleasant emotions that will kill your chances of making a sale.

Salespeople with high EI have patience and aren't pressuring their prospects to make a decision. This means they can continue prospecting with high energy even when they know it will take time to sign the deal. They can easily discern customers' emotional states and can adapt and align their own emotions with that.

Salespeople who have mature levels of EI know how to fine-tune their presentations to pull the right emotional triggers. High-EI salespeople remain positive even amid tons of rejection. They do not take rejections personally and consistently avoid harboring negative emotions.

"No doubt emotional intelligence is more rare than book smarts, but my experience says it is actually more important in the making of a leader. You just can't ignore it," said business titan, the late Jack Welch.

There's a better way than simply pressuring people to buy. When you learn the questioning process we teach, you will transcend the push-pull dynamic with your customers and have them pull you in. They will completely change the way they view you because you've shown them you are customer-focused.

You can ask the right questions at the right time, but if you don't understand the power of your voice, you can still trigger some resistance. But before we move on to discussing how to use that human superpower, we need to make sure we're not still playing reruns of our black-and-white, one-dimensional, non-HDTV version of our sales presentations.

A presentation, as you know, is a prepared (read: rehearsed) talk or Power-Point where you, the salesperson, attempt to grab your prospects' attention and move them toward taking an action step using external motivation techniques such as fear of loss or missing out, greed, guilt, and even envy.

In a typical sales presentation, you're telling your story to a potential customer as if they should care, but guess what? They really don't. You're tossing out a sales pitch to an empty stadium because your assumptions are already putting pressure on them and, well, even science says this isn't very persuasive, but it doesn't take a PhD in science to realize it just ain't working.

When you present or tell your prospects about *your* products or services without first establishing what *their* problems are, if any, the root cause of said problems, and most importantly, how they're affected by them, you automatically cause your prospects to feel tension and sales pressure. You can kiss that sale good-bye right there.

Presentations that begin with you talking about *you* and what *you* think and end with you *hoping* that something, anything, in what you said will trigger a sense of interest that will get your prospects excited about what you sell, are as ubiquitous in sales as JLo and Ben Affleck are in front of paparazzi cameras. We call this "Hopium," an addictive drug that so many salespeople can't seem to quit in which they just hope something they say will lead to a sale. Next time you're jonesing to do this, just say no. Don't do it. Don't take the "Hopium" drug, kids!

A good presentation is key in sales, but it's only about 10 percent of the entire process in our New Model system that's based on knowing precisely what your potential customer wants, why they want it, and how it will make them feel. You can only know that based on the questions you ask them, and before you learn those, let's tap into that superpower called your voice.

Chapter 5

Using the Power of Your Voice

The human voice: It's the instrument we all play. It's the most powerful sound in the world, probably. It's the only one that can start a war or say, "I love you." And yet many people have the experience that when they speak, people don't listen to them.
—Julian Treasure, sound and communication business expert

Y ou talk too much. As a salesperson, you've probably been told that a few times by people who aren't related to you, but let's tweak the verbiage for a second and rephrase it to say that, yes, you're rarely at a loss for words, but better than that, you know exactly how to communicate with others in the most effective way.

You may not be winning any Grammy Awards with that voice, but it is the key to connection with others. When used wisely and appropriately, it can be your greatest asset. When misused, it pushes people away, and we're not talking about your shower rendition of "Stairway to Heaven."

So how does one maximize the power of their voice? According to author and former FBI hostage negotiator Chris Voss, "Your voice alone can be such an art. One of the biggest mistakes people make is using a firm, assertive voice when trying to get their messages across. Instead, use a 'playful voice.'" But hang on a minute. We're not talking about imitating Elmo from *Sesame Street*.

71

Also known by FBI negotiators as the "accommodator's voice," it's a style of speaking that's likable, charming, and relaxed in tone, but still relays the truth. Oh, and although we just quoted a hostage negotiator, we probably don't need to tell you this, but never, ever make your sales prospects feel like they're being held hostage unless, of course, you're selling escape rooms or some sinister new Xbox game.

Verbal Pausing and Verbal Cues

When you carefully consider how you speak and use your voice, you can convey curiosity, collaboration, and interest just by your tone and cadence rather than your words. As a result, you will put your prospects at ease, and they will be more willing to listen to you.

When you speak without pausing, using fillers to sustain momentum, your message can become confusing. A prospect can't just flip on subtitles to understand what you're saying. Learning to slow your pace, inhale while speaking, and insert pauses will turn you into the Streisand or Sinatra of sales—OK, maybe the skilled karaoke versions of them, but you get it—and get people listening. Verbal pausing is a player move in persuasion. "The right word may be effective," Mark Twain said, "but no word was ever as effective as a rightly timed pause."

Next are verbal cues. Think of these as flecks of hot pepper on your pizza; every so often you sprinkle one into the convo to make sure the person you're talking to realizes you are engaged, present, and paying attention:

- *"Right!"*
- *"Tell me more . . ."*
- *"Uh-huh."*
- *"Oh, I see."*
- *"Hmmm . . ."*
- *"Is that right?"*

You can also use body language to communicate. It might feel a little bit over the top at first, and you don't want to go all erratic à la Kramer on *Seinfeld*, but paying attention to your posture, being intentional with facial expressions, and using other nonverbal cues (like nodding while the other person is speaking) can go a long way in helping the client feel heard. It is somewhat different when you are on a call, though not so different in the new Zoom era of meetings, but make sure to implement the other concepts when you aren't face-to-face. It also affects your tonality. If you are on a video call and you're sitting there completely still as if you're in a yoga class or, worse, the Egyptian mummy wing of a museum, you're either going to sound like, well, a corpse, a robot, or, gasp, a telemarketer. So make sure you are nodding when they are speaking, and make sure you are moving your arms and hands as if they were right there in the room watching you, because it all affects how you come across on the call.

Tonality

When people are in a positive frame of mind, they think more quickly and are more likely to collaborate and problem-solve. Positivity creates mental agility in both you and the other person in the conversation. Inflect your voice downward, keeping it calm and slow. This is not a radio ad for a drag race with a guy screaming, "SUNDAY, SUNDAY, SUNDAY!" putting you in the market for a Miracle-Ear as you reach for the mute button.

It's better that you adopt a more natural and neutral tonality with the words you use, fostering a more trusting connection. You want to come off as more human and less salesy, right? Use a calm, relaxed tone, but not too Zen, because you don't want your prospect to start chanting "Ohhhhm" and doing the downward dog. Slow down your pace, have empathy in your voice, and show them that you're there for them as opposed to being there for yourself. Then join hands and sing a few bars of "Kumbaya." Kidding, but you get the picture, right?

In the beginning, this slowing down may not be easy. But learning to slow down and how to use pausing and managing your tone in a way that is far different from what other salespeople do is so worth it. On the flip side, if you sound robotic like you're reading from a script, do you think your prospects will notice this? Yup, they will. Or maybe they won't because they'll be too busy sleeping through your soporific spiel.

Mystery, Surprise, Curiosity

Surprise snags our attention; mystery and curiosity keep it. In Chip and Dan Heath's book *Made to Stick*, they tell us, "The most basic way to get someone's attention is this: Break a pattern." To do this, you need to use the unexpected. Think outside the box but leave the gimmicks for the guys and gals on *Million Dollar Listing*.

In that same book, the authors discuss how Robert Cialdini, Professor Emeritus of Psychology and Marketing at Arizona State University and the author of *Influence: The Psychology of Persuasion*, could keep the attention of his students. Sub in your sales prospects and you've got a similar scenario. Cialdini collected articles on scientific topics and discovered that the articles that best held the interest of his students, read like an episode of *CSI*. Each began with a question and then unfolded like a police investigation. Mysteries are powerful because they create a need for closure. People want answers. Surprises get our attention, sure, but mysteries keep it. And then there's that insatiable curiosity. Human beings are inherently curious.

George Loewenstein, a behavioral economist at Carnegie Mellon University, says curiosity emerges when we notice a gap in our knowledge.[8] These gaps are like open wounds and cause pain, or they're like an itch that needs to be scratched. The only way to kill the pain is to close the gap. Not all gaps are created equally. Think of the worst movie you've ever seen (2018's *Gotti* starring John Travolta is a top contender) and stayed until the end, not because you are a masochist, but because you still want to see what happens.

Curiosity is the intellectual need to answer questions and close patterns. The key is to open gaps first in presenting your ideas, then work to close them; the tendency is to give facts first. The news uses this technique very well: "BREAKING! There's a new drug sweeping the teenage community—and it may be in your own medicine cabinet! This story after these ads."

Most people will sit through the ads just to confirm what drug they are referring to. Same goes for pesky clickbait on the interwebs, where you see a similarly titillating headline and click through a series of ads to find out, well, you were duped and there was no story. Your curiosity, however, led you there. In most cases, a breakthrough is achieved, which leads to a discovery. *Only then* is the answer to the original question revealed.

Tell Your Story

No, no, not your life story, but a compelling, logical, and visual narrative using analogies, anecdotes, or testimonials to which customers can relate easily. Your goal is to have them see themselves in your story. There are six principles you can use to develop a powerful story; you don't have to be a Ted Talk-er or Stephen King to create your own. Actually, let's hope your stories are nothing like King's. Anyway, the principles are as follows:

1. Base it on your unassailable position, meaning the merit of your product or service is undeniable. But not everyone is in the position to say, "Our company is the only one in the world that makes iPhones." So, to establish an unassailable position, you have to have an in-depth understanding of your customers and what is important to them. Then you tailor your product's or service's advantages to their priorities. Questions are the most powerful way to establish your unassailable positioning.

2. Your story should combine facts, features, benefits, questions, and anecdotes. It should also be clear, solid, powerful, and repeatable. Good storytellers engage their audience with body language, tone, eye contact, and emotions. Yep, you're the star in this show, so work it.

3. Your story needs to contain both logic *and* emotion. Facts and figures are great, but they also put people to sleep. Be human. Nick Morgan, author of *Power Cues* says, "In our information-saturated age, business leaders won't be heard unless they're telling stories. Facts and figures and all the rational things that we think are important in the business world actually don't stick in our minds at all. Stories create 'sticky' memories by attaching emotions to things that happen. That means leaders who can create and share good stories have a powerful advantage over others."

4. Base your story on a premise or hypothesis that involves satisfying the customer's needs. Let your story show how your product fits them best, not why the competitor's product is subpar.

Consistent, Persistent Actions

It is true that people listen to the words you speak, but they also pay attention to the actions behind your words. Jerry sees this all the time when training in the pharmaceutical industry. Pharmaceutical sales reps will go in to see a doctor. The doctor will give them two minutes to speak. A great way to implement consistent, persistent actions is to say something along the lines of, "I'm going to make you a promise." Then wait.

A good doctor will usually ask what the promise is. Respond by saying something along the lines of, "I just want to make you a promise, if you don't have much time, that I am not like other salespeople that you've dealt with. When I tell you I'm going to do something, I'm going to do it. I'm not trying to push you to buy anything. I'm trying to see whether we can create value for you. And if we can't, I'll be the first person to say we can't. Now can we get together next week when you have time to have this discussion?" And then stop talking.

What do most salespeople do if they are given two minutes to speak? They rattle off in what we call the machine gun approach. Say everything that you were going to stay in five minutes, but say it in forty-seven seconds and, pull a Pacino in *Scarface* and start screaming, "Say hello to my little friend!" Minus the *Scarface* part, the prospects are listening to absolutely nothing you're saying. Your lips are moving, but they can't hear what you're saying.

Recalibrating Your Communication Skills

Everything has now changed for salespeople and communicators in this unsellable generation. So, what does all this mean for us? Well, the consequences are clear. Regardless of what you sell, the bar for credible communications has been raised higher than SpaceX's all-civilian jaunt into the cosmos.

Awkward sales conversations are nothing new. They've been cringeworthy for eons Fast forward to the 2020s, and ask yourself, are sales conversations comfortable today? Probably not, but they don't have to be so cringey. Hang ups have been around since people actually had phone receivers to slam down. But today, customers aren't uncomfortable, they're kind of just over it, or dare we say, disgusted? The traditional sales communication style absolutely turns the majority of people off quicker than they can hit dismiss.

Decades ago, it wasn't unusual for TV ads to be a few minutes long, or for insurance salespeople to visit us in person. Now, we can click on a banner ad and, hey, presto, we can buy insurance online in a matter of minutes.

We live in a 24/7, three-hundred-plus channel, always connected, online world where countless companies and salespeople are trying to sell us something all the time. Everyone is competing for our attention and our money. If you don't believe us, go do a Google search for puppies. Then log back into your social media accounts and it will look like your pages have been invaded by the puppy gods. There will be so many ads for puppies you never even knew existed, from snickershnizerdoodles and schnauzerpuppers to dogs that look like your Aunt Edna. It's nuts.

In this new post-trust era, we have reduced phone conversations to messages, messages to texts, and texts to symbols and modern-day hieroglyphics known as emojis. Thanks to these technological feats, modern-day salespeople not only have a higher burden of credibility but far less time to build it.

Shake and stir these things together with factors ranging from more information to more complex products, and you have the new digitally fueled modern-day skeptic.

Consumers look at you, the salesperson, very differently than they did in decades past. They challenge your credibility *before* they even listen to what you say. They look for contradictions instead of reasons to believe you. Their defenses are up. They're wiser and ready to assume from the very beginning that you are out to get them, to manipulate them into doing something they don't want to do. They just don't trust you, and guess what? They're not able to buy that trust on Amazon Prime with free, one-day shipping. You have to earn it.

By having a skilled conversation, the prospect will almost always view us as the expert in our field and feel that we are collaborating to solve their problems, not ours. To do this, we need not only be authorities in our field but experts in communication.

According to behavioral science, there are three forms of communication. When it comes to sales, they translate to traditional selling techniques, consultative selling, and dialogue. We've already discussed the first two forms of communication, but the Don Corleone of comms, the one we have yet to discuss, is *dialogue*. This is about having a *skilled* conversation. The prospect is viewing us as the expert in our field and feels that we are collaborating to solve their problems to help them achieve their successful results.

Scientists have proven that we are the most persuasive when we allow others to persuade themselves. We are the *least* persuasive when we tell people things or attempt to dominate, posture, or push them into doing something. Those with children may be acutely aware of this when asking them to clean their rooms, though perhaps that's not the best analogy because it's hard to imagine kids persuading themselves to, all of a sudden, start sprucing up their hot messes. That being said, when we alter our way of communicating using the connection between human behavior and the concepts of persuasion, we will see better results and it won't be nearly as maddening as trying to persuade the kids to pick up their mountains of mess.

Unfortunately, the majority of salespeople were originally taught to sell by presenting, telling, spewing facts and data, and persuading—no, pushing. So the sales training that is continually being spread like gospel is proven to be the least persuasive. Moreover, it works against human psychology. You don't need to study neuroscience like Jeremy did to know that it just doesn't work.

When you tell your partner, spouse, or kid they need to do something you want them to do, what's the typical response? The sound of crickets and an over-flowing garbage can, right? The concept of persuasion doesn't directly benefit them as they see it; it primarily benefits you. Though, regarding that garbage can, it's hard to imagine how taking that stinkin' thing out won't benefit all, but, alas, human nature.

We are teaching you the skills needed to sell more by exploring how human beings make decisions and how and why people are or are not persuaded. Why not learn how to sell using something that works *with* human behavior instead of going *against* it?

We've already established that people buy on emotion but justify that purchase with logic or at least their version of logic. The New Model of Selling provides you with a sequence of questions that are more persuasive, create a more safe environment, and contain less pressure. It's about no longer trying to push people into doing something you want them to do. The only way to open a customer's mind is to *connect* with them. It doesn't matter if you have all the right questions or the best pitch. If you don't communicate it effectively, you can push them away.

Do you feel the burn of rejection when people respond negatively to you while talking to them about your solution? Do you sometimes get frustrated because you can't get your point across? If you answered yes to either of these questions, most of your frustration probably resides in the way we have been taught to communicate. Telling and persuading tend to be self-focused, and, as such, this doesn't connect with most of us. Traditional or old selling techniques are all about the first form of communication.

With AIDA model techniques, the salesperson would come into the office or home of the potential customer and try to find something they have in common. Back in the day, it worked. People felt connected to their sales representatives. However, this tactic has been as overplayed as Journey's "Don't Stop Believin'" at your neighborhood karaoke bar.

If you use this model, people will know what you're going to say before you even say it. Mind-numbing, time-wasting chitchat *never* feels authentic.

Breakdown of a Sales Conversation

Contrast this with the best sales experience you've had as a customer. Did the sales rep ask you the same robotic, rote questions, or did they facilitate an actual conversation with you? Did you learn something new in the convo? Now think about that time you were buying something, and the associate used the old model. Were you silently begging for the conversation to end? Looking for the exits to flee? That reaction is common during the first 10 percent of time spent with a prospect. Not good if your prospect is jumping ship while the band, a.k.a. your sales approach, drones on.

The next 10 percent would be about identifying needs. First, the salesperson asks a few generic questions such as: "Can you tell me two to three problems that you're experiencing now and how you'd like to fix those problems?" The prospect would then rattle off a few generic problems to the salesperson, with simple logical answers that are just the surface of what is really going on.

Then the salesperson goes into their presentation all about the features and benefits of their product or service. They speak about how great their company is, and that they have the best this and the best that, which, by the way, every salesperson says, am I right? This part comprises 50 percent of the outdated sales model. By this point, your prospect is probably having a mental debate over whether to eat a healthy salad for lunch or a fast food fried chicken sandwich. The struggle is real.

Then during the last 30 percent of the sale, they go in for the close, and what happens? The prospect, if they're even still awake or there at all, throws out objections. Then the salesperson must scrounge to overcome their objections and try to close them again and again. (Don't worry, we'll talk about objection handling in chapter 10.) At this point, the salesperson starts to chase them to try to convince them to purchase. Seems a little desperate, no? That's because it is!

Let's look at the composition of time spent on each activity.

- Ten percent on building trust.
- Ten percent on identifying needs.
- Fifty percent on giving the presentation.
- Thirty percent on asking for the sale and dealing with objections.

So, as you can see here, only about 10 percent of the time is spent building trust.

The New Model gets people to think the *right* way about selling. Once they have the correct mindset, they can take the time, effort, and energy to learn. How do you learn these ideas that make conversations comfortable for people? After all, a conversation is merely an exchange of information between people. By having a conversation, we are not putting the sale in the customer's hands; we are *partnering* with the customer to see whether value can be added.

Words Matter

As Mark Twain once noted, "The difference between the almost right word and the right word is really a large matter—'tis the difference between the lightning-bug and the lightning." Words also elicit feelings in human beings. By choosing how you frame and talk about something, you are causing others to think about it in a specific way. A person's perspective can drastically change by the words you choose to use. Choose words that show people you're producing a safe environment for them. Safe environments lead to major sales success.

Your ability to create a low-pressure, safe environment with words and language that fuse logic and emotion into a comforting cocktail is crucial to smashing sales!

One of the most powerful things that we ever learned from business trainer Jeffrey Gitomer is that most sales happen in a relaxed atmosphere. Think about it: have you ever been rushing out of your local drug store only to be stopped by a newspaper salesperson trying to sell you a subscription? "Free umbrella if you sign up today!" How many times have you stopped to subscribe right there on the spot? Probably never. Unless it was torrentially pouring down and you really needed that umbrella, right?

Unfortunately, salespeople also often inadvertently shut the customer's mind with what we call hard words. Rather than use words like, "You should," "You want to," or "This is perfect for you," think of saying things like, "You *might* want to," "This *might* possibly work for you," "This looks like it might be a decent fit," or "What are your thoughts?"

You want to use words that always make the customer aware that this is *their* decision. Hard words and hard phrases, like, "You should," "You must," or "You have to," sound biased, presumptuous and, frankly, obnoxious. And if a prospect or a customer feels like we're biased, presumptuous, and obnoxious, they're outta there faster than you can say, "But wait, there's more!" Soft words or "neutral languaging," as Jeremy coined it, lets the customer know that they're in charge, and that we're not trying to embellish anything. We're sending the signal with soft words that this is their decision, and in the final analysis, it *is* their decision.

With traditional techniques, the salesperson would come into the potential customer's office or home and find something they have in common. They would talk about the weather, or maybe they would see a picture of the client fishing and talk about how they like to fish—basically talking about a bunch of topics that really have nothing to do with why they're there. The salesperson would invest all their energy on this futile fishing expedition of their own, trying to connect. It's hit or miss and most of all, it's exhausting. Do you pick up on this when a salesperson is trying to sell you something? We do want to look for common ground, but *after* the business conversation, when we have built a level of trust.

As you can see illustrated here, traditional selling often looks very much like this: a mere 10 percent of the time is about building trust and listening to prospects. Is this you? If it is, don't worry, we'll work on that.

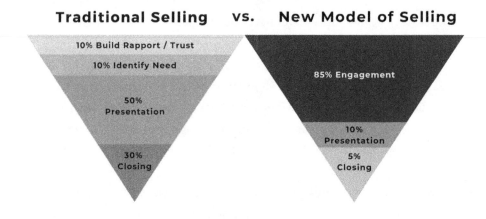

Traditional Selling   vs.   New Model of Selling

10% Build Rapport / Trust

10% Identify Need

85% Engagement

50% Presentation

10% Presentation

30% Closing

5% Closing

In the New Model of Selling, eighty-five percent of time with prospects is spent on engagement, listening and building trust. Just 10 percent is spent on presenting, and a mere 5 percent on committing or closing. We will discuss this in more detail later when we cover the actual questions to ask so you connect early in the sales conversation.

Chapter 6

Listen and Learn

The best way to persuade people is with your ears—by listening to them.
—Dean Rusk, Secretary of State under LBJ and JFK

S o you're a good talker, an enviable orator. And that's great. But you're not here to wow people with inspirational speeches and TEDx Talks. If you don't know how to *listen* intently, you'll likely never find out what you're supposed to say, what to ask, or when to seek clarification. While some salespeople don't know how to communicate and connect effectively, even fewer know how to listen.

A case study of sixteen thousand people stated that 95 percent of customers think that sales reps talk too much. That's a problem. It also found that 86 percent of customers think that sales reps ask the wrong questions.[9] That means that only 14 percent are asking the right questions. People who ask questions to set the customer up are not seeking understanding; they're seeking to fulfill their own agenda. Your goal should be to be a part of that sparse 5 percent of sales folk who customers think don't talk too much. Squad goals, indeed, but perfectly attainable!

Rick Phillips, the author of *Effective Communication Skills* says, "There are no uninteresting people in the world, only disinterested listeners." The irony of any sales interaction is that, while we want our customers to listen to what we have to say, quite often, we are unconsciously unwilling to reciprocate the courtesy. You still there? Good. If you're struggling with a customer, perhaps it's time to listen to them to sell more.

Psychologist and one of the founders of the humanistic and client-centered approach in psychology, Carl Rodgers, once said, "A person's inability to communicate is a result of the failure to listen effectively, skillfully, and with *understanding* of another person." Hearing is one thing, and it can oftentimes be very selective (see: spouse, partner, or kids somehow "not hearing" your pleas to take out that growing mountain of garbage), but listening is a complex physical process that's very natural and passive.

Listening to our customers is imperative! Listening requires discipline, energy, and effort. It's estimated that successful salespeople spend as much as 70 percent of their day listening. However, on average, people are about 25 percent effective listeners in terms of what they remember and what they apply. Now, if we're only 25 percent effective where we spend 70 percent of our time, it makes sense to place a premium on improving that skill.

Shari Kulkis, account manager at Genentech, says, "I think listening skills are really the Achilles' Heel of salespeople—especially young folks." Retired Northern Illinois University Professor of Sales Dan Weilbaker would know, and he agrees. "I give a lot of verbal directions and assignments for the students to realize they have to listen to get it right, and to understand what I'm saying. I don't ask them, 'Do you understand?' They have two options," he explains.

"One, they can come ask me about it, or they can go ahead and do what they think they need to do. If they do what they think they need to do and it's wrong, that is going to impact their grade. Most students will complain, and I will use that opportunity to reinforce that they didn't listen. You need to listen, and if you don't understand, you ask."

Listening to your potential customer is sometimes confused with recognizing the connections between the customer's thoughts and your own. What you already know cannot be subtracted from what you need to hear from your prospect. Even if you know 90 percent of the customer's story, you need to hear 100 percent. The questions you need to ask are more than likely in the 10 percent of the information you don't know, y'know?

All that, "What you don't know won't hurt you" stuff? Toss it out. Like *The Handmaid's Tale* author Margaret Atwood wrote in *The Blind Assassin*, it's "A dubious maxim: sometimes what you don't know can hurt you very much."

Take this scenario:

> **Prospect:** *"We are going through a major restructuring of the entire company. Our CEO just retired. Now our VP of sales is taking over . . ."*
>
> The **Average Salesperson** might say: *"I know that. I read that in the* Wall Street Journal *yesterday."*

What do you think the prospect will think? *Oh, this salesperson is so intelligent, I don't have to tell him much, so we can save time?* Or *What could this outsider possibly know about what's going on inside my company? The restructure affects me, not you.*

Even if you already know everything the prospect tells you, it's not the same as being told by them because the information belongs to the customer; psychologically, you want them to feel all the feels that come with the admission or to uncover the reality your question just illuminated. Sometimes they need to say it out loud to fully paint the picture in their own mind—to have the cartoon bubble above their head show a lightning bulb when they finally come to the conclusion on their own!

If the customer is likely to buy in, there needs to be an intense pull to solve their problem with your solution. No matter the root of the need, there should be urgency. But don't confuse urgency with alarmism. You don't want to scare them away. The only way to create that sense of immediacy without seeming like an alarmist is by completely understanding the relationship between the client as problem revealer and you, the salesperson, as problem solver.

Take a look at this scenario:

> **Prospect:** *"What our problem really boils down to, is that we lose a lot of time just getting our product line in and out of our warehouses."*
>
> **Average Salesperson:** *"It sounds like you need to get your hands on a bunch of these new forklifts we just came out with. Let me tell you about our new model . . ."*

There is a clear progression of ideas here, from the warehouse to loading the product line to the forklift. And while the forklift will probably solve the prospect's problem, it's not part of the customer's story. The salesperson is butting in and assuming it is, when, in all reality, it might be something *completely* different.

The salesperson may as well say, *"We'll come back to what you were saying after I get my 'sales pitch' out of the way"* before being shown the door.

Listening for clues in the customer's story to begin a sales pitch is another misguided way of attempting to connect the potential customer's thoughts with the salesperson's. It's like meeting someone for the first time and they start to say, "I like chocolate . . ." and you excitedly interject and say, "Me too" before finding out that the person's sentence continued with "covered ants." Would you prefer those bugs in white, dark, or milk chocolate?

Listening is a mode of selling, yes, but for listening to be truly effective, other modes of selling, such as talking about features and benefits, must be switched *off* if you want to go from getting average results to becoming a top 1 percent earner in your industry.

Now that we know how *not* to listen, let's discuss how to do it better. You listening?

Open Listening

Open listening—which is listening without judging—focusing on the other person, and putting aside your agenda of making the sale are so powerful that they will completely differentiate you from any other salesperson. Linda Richardson, best-selling author of *Changing the Sales Conversation,* said, "Listening has always been important. Think about listening today as *close listening*. It is your ability to be *mindful* in the moment, so that you can demonstrate attention and gain full comprehension of what your customer has shared with you."[10]

But do we listen to our prospects? Based on our experience of training thousands of people, we don't. Rude, we know, but not intentionally, and no more. Listening requires you to do something that most salespeople flat out don't do. It requires you to let go of your need to think about what you will say next and let your natural self take over. It's like taking pictures. Some people are naturally photogenic, but if you're not a supermodel or supermodel's spawn, perhaps you know what we're talking about.

When you deliberately pose for a picture, you may come off looking, well, posed, possibly awkward, and a candidate for all the filters used by Madonna and the Kardashians combined. A candid shot, however, assuming it's totally SFW, oftentimes comes off more naturally, more lifelike, with no filters needed. Listening is similar, minus the filters. Turn those off. If we are not disciplined to listen, we will be far more inclined to prepare our response, which comes off as canned, rather than hear what our prospects are saying and respond more naturally.

Listening also requires you to decipher the meaning beyond the words being uttered. Proper and purposeful listening forces you to slow down before firing off quick questions or propelling your pitch. When you slow down, your questions have better quality, leading to a much better conversion that triggers the prospect to want to open up even more.

Lucky for you, listening is like the Jan Brady of sales—it gets little recognition from your fellow salespeople. The Marcia, Marcia, Marcia of sales is the sales spiel. And that's all well and good, but because listening is not identified with selling, listening remains the advantage of the salesperson who uses the New Model of Selling. So your secret is safe. You are not likely to be out-listened by other salespeople in your industry. The sharpest competitive edge is the one your competitors don't want and don't understand. Take that, Marcia.

On the flip side, lazy listening dilutes your communication power, especially because you are likely to ask questions based on the wrong information gathered while you were slacking off, neither present nor listening, into a distracted wasteland. Hashtag huge sales fail.

Know What to Listen for by Becoming a CEO

At some point in your career, you may have thought, *If I were the CEO, this is what I would have done.* Here is your chance to partake in some CEO cosplay. Be your own chief executive officer—become an active and effective listener by utilizing clues, essence, and opportunities—the top-shelf trio of total sales success.

Clues, Essence, and Opportunities

What are you supposed to listen for when a customer responds to you? The answer is simple. You listen for those three things, the Peter, Paul, and Mary of CEOdom:

clues, essence, and opportunities. If you focus your listening skills on these three areas, you will unlock that firewall and gain further insights into what will hopefully become your very loyal customer.

Clues

Clues are those things your significant other drops when they want something. Clueless is you when you miss those clues and forget the important date or occasion. Clues are also words or phrases that a customer provides when responding to you and your questions. They may not even be aware they are sharing this information, but the astute listener looks for meaning beyond the words and recognizes that what the person says (or does not say) is chock-full-o-clues, some more useful than others.

Often the clues are triggers. Not to be confused with social media speak in which it's something that provokes a, shall we say, passionate or heated reaction, a trigger in sales is something that will generate a follow-up *question*. Clues can be almost anything—for word nerds, they can be adjectives, adverbs, or words that convey vagueness and ambiguity. For the rest of us, they're just hints that require further clarification to properly understand what, exactly, our customer means.

For example, a customer may say, *"It is critical that these patients get to a goal."*

The *typical* salesperson will jump all over that statement and will likely respond with a laundry list of reasons why their product is the right solution for getting to the goal. The *great* salesperson will hear the word "critical" and know that critical could have many different meanings. So a follow-up question to this clue would be very appropriate.

"Doctor, I can only imagine how important it is to get these patients to goal. Can you share with me why it is so critical? Why did you choose that particular word?"

Clues can also be nonverbal, conveyed by body language or facial expressions, which are easy to spot when we're paying attention. For example, when the customer says, *"It is critical that these patients get to their goal,"* and they jab a finger onto a hard surface, it could mean that they are adding extra emphasis to convey how important this issue is to them. Your follow-up question may be:

"By your body language, it appears that this is something that is vitally important to you. Can you share with me why it is so critical?"

Or you could ask it this way: *"Based on your body language, that seems very important to you. What's behind that?"*

If the customer places extra emphasis on the word "goal" with their tone or pitch, it may indicate that, yep, goals are very important to this customer. A follow-up question may be: *"You seem to be very focused on the goal for these patients. Can you share with me why getting them to their goal is so critical in your experience?"* Or you could ask it this way: *"Why is getting them to their goal so important to you now, though?"*

Emotions are a big trigger and can be conveyed in many ways, though hopefully not in a crying or hissy fit because at the end of the day, you're in sales, not psychiatry. Auditory signals and body language can convey emotions very easily. If a client punches a hole in the wall, however, the problems are clearly out of your wheelhouse.

We're talking a tap on the table, a point of the finger, an increase in speaking volume, or just words. Adjectives to describe words or phrases can be powerful clues to your customer's emotions about a particular subject or thought. Remember that customers buy emotionally and defend their decision logically.

If you are actively listening and can uncover an emotion within the words they use, you can react to this emotion in your response. Great sales specialists want to tap into that emotional reservoir and harvest the true feelings behind emotional clues. The active listener knows the value of paying attention to clues. They're not going to hit you over the head—at least we hope not.

Essence

Essence is the intent or true meaning behind the words or phrases your customer uses. As studies confirm, most customers think salespeople don't ask good questions, and they're thinking correctly. And why is this? Because they're probably not paying attention. If customers come in with this mindset by default and feel that sales specialists don't really care about what they say, you'll be waiting a long time to stumble upon any of their words with deeper meaning, and no, it doesn't depend on what your definition of "the words or phrases" is. Customers may not even be intentionally replying with empty words but do this subconsciously.

The average salesperson interprets what a person says without asking for clarity. However, the better sales specialist realizes that filters are being used that can confuse what is being communicated. While filters may be an aging pop star's or social media starlet's best friend, filters in sales can be tricky to recognize. These filters can include the speaker's or listener's background, environment, culture, emotions, gender, age, previous experiences, hearsay, and assumptions.

Our goal in selling is to truly *understand* our customers. How do we accomplish this? By focusing on learning what our customers truly mean—by gaining clarity about what they say. The purpose of gaining clarity is twofold: First, it is a way to ensure that our customers understand what *we* said—the essence of what we are trying to communicate. And second, it provides reassurance that we are genuinely interested in our customers and the thoughts they are sharing. After all, we care enough to ask those follow-up questions, right?

There are three basic ways to clarify something you have heard.

- Question
- Paraphrase
- Summarize

Despite the fact that you may have been told as a child not to answer a question with a question; in sales, it is perfectly acceptable to respond to a question with another question—especially a clarifying question. Just don't let the kids hear this because you'll be on the interrogation line until they go to college. But really, how else can you understand what your customer intends to say and eliminate confusion?

To paraphrase is to put into your own words what you believe the customer said. When you choose different words to communicate the same idea, it provides clarity and communicates to the customer that you are genuinely interested in what they are saying. When you summarize, you review the conversation from the customer's frame of reference (not yours). The rule of thumb of essence is "don't assume, ask."

Opportunities

Like people and Air Jordans, opportunities come in all sizes, some much bigger than others and others tiny, adorable baby-sized, but the one thing they have in common is that they, unlike the hard-to-find Jordans, thankfully arise in many conversations with customers. Often our customers' statements contain hidden opportunities.

For example, if you sold medical device equipment, in the course of a conversation with the sales rep, the physician may happen to mention that they are going to a meeting next month in Boston. Viewing this as an opportunity, the astute salesperson can call a friend or colleague in Boston to get the names of some of the city's highly coveted restaurants or hotspots. During their next interaction, the savvy sales rep can conveniently name-drop some of them to the physician. "My rep in Boston says you must check out this amazing new, off-the-beaten-path ramen spot," you suggest.

This small act, which didn't cost anything (except for time), sends a powerful message to the doctor. It communicates that we were listening to what the physician told us and that we remembered this after our discussion and took the time and effort to seek out information that could be helpful. It is a way to build trust and appreciation. Bonus points for reservation hook-ups too.

Opportunities at times can be rather obvious. Your customer can share a story about a colleague who happens to be their golfing buddy. Or opportunities can be more subtle: an award hanging on a wall in a remote part of the office. Opportunities can be spoken or seen. It's all about *paying attention* to what our customers say (a.k.a. listening to them) and to the surrounding environment.

Listening Tips

Be Aware and Present

Have you ever been in the middle of what you thought was a deep conversation with someone, and they start reading and replying to a text message in the middle of your conversation? What about when you're sharing a crazy story with a group of friends about an experience you had, and someone comes up and breaks in with their own story?

Unfortunately, most of us can relate. How did these experiences make you feel? Did you feel annoyed, infuriated, or frustrated? Did you feel that it was total disrespect that invalidated what you were trying to say? Bottom line is, and you don't need to be an etiquette expert here, it's just plain rude. So, so rude. Insert angry face emoji here.

Now, consider what the other person communicated to you by their actions. That they were not *present* in the conversation and that they're also rude. It's easy to see the situation as the fault of the other person and condemn them, but hang on a minute; take a long, hard look at yourself. Have *you* ever done any of these things when you were with a potential customer? Were you ever not present in the conversation? It's OK; you can admit it. Most of us are guilty, and if you are too, it's time to break that habit.

Even if you think you've only done it once or twice, it could happen more than you think, so try to stay conscious of your behaviors in conversations as you practice these advanced listening skills. Being present and aware enables your brain to gather information from what the potential customer says. Not every customer is the same. They all have unique needs and cannot all be bought with the same exact questions. They all, however, can be turned off by your disinterest or lack of focus.

Be Curious

Have you ever been venting to someone and gotten angry when they immediately told you how to fix your problem? Even if their solution makes sense, it's off-putting to be hit with an instant, presumptive solution to your problem, and it comes off as someone telling you what to do instead of just listening to how you feel. Even if the other person is right, no one likes to be told what to do. Also, when it comes to listening to your problems, a high-speed answer isn't always the best one and, dare we say, a dial-up response is more thoughtful and contemplative.

Instant solution-based answers to problems are constructed on very little information about what is going on. They don't consider what action might have already been taken. In fact, they don't consider much. How do you think you might have felt if, instead of them coming up with a solution quickly, they asked you to expound on what you were saying? How would you have felt if they asked you more questions about your problem, what caused the problem, and how it affected you?

You probably would have felt like this person understood what had happened to you, and you might have even opened up to them *more* about your situation.

It's the same with your potential customers. So, as hard as it may be, remember to keep your statements and solutions at bay until it's appropriate to bring them into the conversation. Then, let your prospect flesh out their problems with the skilled questions you ask them.

Be Silent and Pause

So many salespeople will ask a prospect a question, and if the prospect doesn't answer in a split second, they will jump in to answer the question for them, change the subject, or even start asking other questions. Make. It. Stop. *Now.* Never do this, ever, because if you do, you can kiss that (non) customer goodbye. When you do this, it makes your potential customer feel invalidated.

When you become more open, your prospect will become more open to you as well, and they'll tell you the truth. Say goodbye to the antiquated real estate and sales mantra that "Buyers are liars." Also delete the last sentence of that mantra that says, "Sellers are worse." Old school. Toss it.

When you ask a question, be silent and be comfortable with that silence. This is not a date where silence is awkward. Being quiet is not a trick or a closing technique either. It is simply respectful and courteous. It allows your prospect to reflect on the questions before answering them. The first answers your potential customer gives you are just the first layer of the onion.

As you ask them deeper questions, you'll see that their answers become more truthful, more revealing, and more emotional. Allow your potential customer to answer the questions you ask. This isn't a cable TV news network where people are talking over each other. Never interrupt to answer with questions. Never change the subject. Silence equals sales.

Be Understanding

Have you ever had someone tell you something that you felt was completely wrong and went against everything you believed in? Maybe it was something you knew from your own experience to be wrong, so you started debating and arguing with that person? Welcome to social media and modern-day politics. And as you may have noticed, it neither resolves anything, nor does it change that person's opinions as much as you wish it would.

Have you ever handled a prospect's objection with a *"Yes, but . . ."* answer to try to persuade them over to your way of thinking? How many of those debates did you win? Did you ever feel the other person changed their point of view to yours? If you did manage to do that, maybe you need to write a book of your own.

What do you think might happen if, despite your desire to be right, you actually listened to the other person? What could happen if you asked them deeper questions to expand on where they were coming from and why they felt that way? What if you did all of this without judgment and without injecting your interpretation and opinion into the conversation?

Any of the following scenarios could happen:

- You will probably gain much more understanding of where they are coming from.
- The other person might subconsciously question their own way of thinking as they listen to themselves answer your skilled questions.
- It might actually make them reconsider their point of view.
- They will likely be more open to listening to you and your way of thinking.

In the book *The 7 Habits of Highly Effective People,* Stephen Covey said, "Seek first to understand, then to be understood." Listening and accepting another's point of view does not mean that you must alter your mind and your beliefs. Newsflash: you don't have to agree with someone to listen to them.

On the contrary, when you suspend your assumptions about how you view the world, your prospects will be more than willing to listen to you and your point of view because you'll seem knowledgeable, accepting, nonjudgmental, and fascinating because frankly, in this day and age, being this way is as rare as a hip-hop artist who doesn't use Auto-Tune.

If you want your potential customers to change, you may want to change how *you* approach them. You can literally listen your prospects into changing by staying open to them with a desire to be understanding.

Always ask for clarity. You don't want things to get lost in translation. What you interpret as one meaning may be completely different from the actual meaning. Too many sales are lost because salespeople assume that they know and understand their potential customers' problems when they really don't.

The second key is to accept without judging and interjecting your interpretation. Don't judge others by your own perception of reality. When you judge, you are not changing the other person. By judging, you're only demonstrating your need to criticize and undermine others. Judge Judy gets paid the big bucks to do that. You'll make yours by operating in a judgment-free forum.

Try this: the next time someone doesn't immediately drive forward when the light turns green at a stoplight, don't honk your horn. Just sit and give them some room. This might be hard if you are in a hurry or if you're in a busy metropolis where people pound on the horn if you don't move in a nanosecond but try it—carefully, of course. Although the guy behind you may not appreciate it, you will likely experience a reduction in your own emotional emissions.

Do it, and things like it, enough and you'll experience a massive difference in your happiness, health, and stress levels. Besides, you don't really know why they didn't move when the light turned green, do you? Maybe they were distracted because they had a screaming child in the back seat, or maybe they were just having a bad day.

Give your ego and your own experiences an extended lunch and a long nap afterward. Remember: don't tell people you know how they feel. Chances are you don't. It is just your interpretation. Instead, ask them *how* that made them feel. Turn it into a question and reap the rewards.

Many people view therapists as natural problem solvers. However, they don't have all the answers. You don't go to therapy and walk out with a checklist on how to live your life, as convenient as that may sound. They don't give you *all* the answers. You have to find your own answers. A good therapist's job is to ask the right questions. Self-discovery is all part of the process. As Gandhi said, "The best way to find yourself is to lose yourself in the service of others." But enough about the self-help. That's on another bookshelf.

As sales therapists—er, salespeople—we must do the same thing. Let them find themselves in your service. Never assume you have the solution. Instead, work your way through the conversation and have the customer come to that conclusion on their own. As you'll see, it's the most mutually beneficial banter in business you'll ever have.

Chapter 7
Sequence of Questions

Solutions come through evolution. They come through asking the right questions because the answers pre-exist. It is the questions that we must define and discover. You don't invent the answer—you reveal the answer.
—Jonas Salk

OK, so you know how to speak. You understand how to listen. You may think you're ready to bust out of the gate but hold your horses for a second. As George Bernard Shaw, famously said, "The single biggest problem in communication is the illusion that it has taken place." Do you know the exact questions you should be asking? And do you know *how* to ask those questions?

The truth is, you can be a great communicator, but if you don't know what to ask, you're only going to hold your audience for so long unless you're Barbara Walters, who used to ask her celebrity interviewees what kind of trees they identified with. That kept our interest because it was such a bizarro question you had to stick around to hear the answer. In sales, however, skip the sequoias and go straight for the sequence. The sequence of questions we provide creates a logical and coherent structure you and your sales team can use to generate meaningful dialogue.

For example, in the traditional version of the sequence of questions, the salesperson only has to identify a possible customer, determine whether they're qualified, make the pitch, close the sale, and provide ongoing support. At each step in the process, the salesperson knows exactly what needs to be done next.

But let's not get ahead of the process. Before we tell you what questions to ask, you need to know how to create a powerful opening using some of our previously shared methods. We've discovered how to take the concepts and ideas we have—the quintessential way to think like a customer—and break down the sales process to get the customer to do their own thinking.

Interest-Generating Opening

Openings are words that begin the business portion of the discussion. Some customers prefer to start with small talk about their weekend, sports, kids, or other personal revelations, but there is a time to discuss business during every sales conversation.

Customers are preoccupied. They're distracted. They're on data overload. We're willing to bet they're probably not excited to see a salesperson unless said salesperson already has a relationship with them, and even then, that's debatable at times. The bottom line is you must be able to trigger your prospects' minds to want to open up to you and want to engage with you and do it rather quickly.

One of the things we have to remember is that opening the call is different from a greeting. A greeting is not an opening. If you say, "How was your weekend?" That's a greeting. It's not an opening. An opening is the beginning of your sales conversation—your first *business* words.

Now that we've differentiated the two, it's really important to have a strong transition between a greeting and an opening. Non sequiturs are almost always awkward. It's like going from "Did you catch the latest episode of *Ted Lasso*?" straight to "Now tell me about your patients' needs for diarrhea meds."

To transition successfully, you have to capture interest quickly. A squirrel has an attention span of about one second. A goldfish's attention span is nine seconds. The human attention span is said to be ten to twelve seconds (though in this age of Insta TikToking, it's probably less), plus you want to remember the eight-second rule so prospects will be open to listening to you.

Time is of the essence, and we don't have a lot of it to get mental access. Just because we have physical access doesn't mean that we have mental access. So, if a customer doesn't listen, nothing else matters. And that's why capturing interest quickly is crucial to making any sales interaction meaningful not just for us but also for them.

There are five key principles to developing a prospective customer's interest:

1. Research to find interesting ways to open the dialogue. Say you sell mattresses; instead of putting your prospects to sleep on them—which actually isn't a bad idea—dazzle your prospects with a fascinating factoid like: "Today, only 12 percent of people dream in black and white—the rest of us dream in color. Before color television, just 15 percent of people dreamed in color."

2. Use openings that create safe environments. For example, "We do business with a lot of companies and we're proud of our work and our clients get amazing results, but that doesn't necessarily mean we're right for you. Before we go over how we might be able to help you, can I ask you a few questions around XYZ?"

3. Bring value to the interaction before you start the sales conversation. Let's say you read a newspaper article about issues a prospect's company is having with salespeople not making any sales, and you have this very book in your hands, so you say, "I saw in the paper that you guys might be having some issues making sales and I thought you might like to read this book."

4. Make connections that can help the customer. "I ran into Elle Woods the other day and realized it might make sense for you to meet her because her company . . ."

5. Be crystal clear about what you need to know and go about finding it. Prep for every sales conversation by asking yourself, "What do I want to know and what do I want to share?" Be prepared to discuss information about yourself, your product, your services, and your industry. "By failing to prepare, you are preparing to fail," said a wise man known as Benjamin Franklin.

Intent, Content, Condition

Genuine curiosity drives us to seek understanding. This incorporates the entire architecture of a great question: intent, content, and condition.

Intent is simply figuring out why you are asking this question. You don't need to ask a question that you already know the answer to unless said question is going to help your prospect relive the pain of their problem. Your intent is always to seek *understanding*.

You don't want to ask leading questions. Ask questions to uncover some information you want to learn or need to know. Remember, time is precious and it's ticking, so you do need to spend it wisely here.

Content is discovering *what* exactly you want to know. There are times when salespeople will beat around the bush or infuse so much ambiguity or vagueness into their questions that they confuse the customer. A confused customer may end up being no customer. Write down specifically what you want to know. More often than not, you will find that what you write down can be the catalyst for a well-crafted question.

Condition involves deciphering how the question will land with the customer. Sorta like a comedian trying out his jokes on Twitter, this step is critical to improving the quality of your questions. Ask your question aloud so you can hear what you are saying. If you were the customer, how would that question make you feel? Would it put you on the defensive? Leave you feeling confused? Make you feel as if you were being set up? If the answer is yes to any of these, you need to rework the question. By putting yourself in your customer's mind and actually *listening* to your own question, you'll save yourself from bombing the sale.

Asking the right questions creates a safe environment because you give the customer permission to feel safe enough to open up to you about what their real problems and objectives are. The customer will likely share with you truthfully what's been holding them back. Your questions should encourage thought and dialogue. A series of questions will best provide you with a true understanding of the customer. Great questions will lead the customer to their own conclusions, and that arrival translates to your arrival as a sales success story!

Watch what happens when your prospects start listening to themselves answering your questions. They start to process the information internally as they are talking. Their answers help them think about their problems and to own the idea that they want to solve those problems. As they consciously and subconsciously internalize what they are saying to you, their answers help them look at and challenge their beliefs as to why they keep allowing their present situation to continue.

When you ask these questions and people tell you their problems, they are also telling themselves why they have those problems, what's causing those problems, the root cause of them, and how important it is for them to change their problems.

People will start saying to themselves things like: *"Why do I keep putting off buying life insurance for my family?" "Why do I keep investing my money with this firm; maybe I should look at what this guy is going over with me—maybe I could possibly get a higher return?" "Why do I keep commuting to work an hour each way when I could be like this lady working from my home?"* or *"Wow, why do I keep advertising my business this way when I could be getting leads that have higher conversions for my sales team?"*

They will keep questioning themselves. *"What's preventing me from doing this? What's holding me back?"* They will question why they allow themselves to stay in that same situation. Then, they will start to think about doing something to change their situation. When your potential clients get to this point thanks to your impressive questioning skills, they will start to persuade themselves that they're ready to make that change now, not in six months, or a year, but right now.

In sales, you must learn *specific* questions and *when* and *how* to ask them in a step-by-step structure that will get your prospects to sell themselves rather than you trying to do it. That's where we come in.

The questions we're referring to are intended to bring out people's internal and external truths and, most importantly, their emotions. It's not about you talking to them. Rather, it's them talking about themselves to you.

Here's a snippet of what the process looks like and what the questions will focus on:

1. Connection Questions: These questions take the focus away from you and put the focus on your potential customer.
2. Situation Questions: These questions help you find out what their present situation is.

3. Problem Awareness Questions: What problems do they have, if any, what caused them, and how are they affecting them?

4. Solution Awareness Questions: These questions involve your prospect and their idea, which causes them to emotionally attach themselves to solving their problem and doing that *with* you while seeing what their future will look like once the problem is solved.

5. Consequence Questions: These questions help them question their way of thinking and explore the consequences of not changing their situation.

6. Qualifying Questions: These questions confirm how important it is for them to change their situation.

7. Transition Questions: These questions help you naturally transition into going over how your solution will help them solve their problem. These questions give you the correct setup to present your solution at the right time.

Do you think most of your potential customers would be open to listening to you? Uh, yah, of course they will, and you know what? A very interesting thing will happen. Are you ready? Wait for it. OK, here goes: Your potential client will like you! They will start calling you back and chasing you for a change. Now, that's a novel concept we can all get behind, no?

Over the next few chapters, we are going to break down the questioning process and how you can begin implementing it into your business and sales conversations.

Chapter 8

To Sell or Not to Sell, That Is the Question

The wise man doesn't give the right answers, he poses the right questions.
—Claude Lévi-Strauss, French anthropologist

Now is the time to modernize your sales process or risk becoming irrelevant. Living in a world where things change, upgrade, downgrade, and evolve by the second, there's no time like right now to do this, especially considering that, in the time you took to read this book, there are probably fifty new upgrades to your smartphone. Without a reliable, *modern* template to follow, along with knowledge of sales stages, you and your sales team will underperform. It's like trying to play an MP3 file on your uncle's vintage boom box.

The sales process acts as a road map and guide. If the road map you've been using keeps leading you down dead ends, it's time to do something different. The sales methods that worked for you in the past may not generate the same response right now. And what's working today may not work tomorrow. You get the point. The sales game is fluid, so you must take this approach too.

When it comes to sales, intent is *everything*. Your intent is your state of mind at the time of your action. Ask yourself two things: "What's my purpose?" and "What do I plan to do?" Motivational speaker Brian Tracy suggests, "The first thing you should feed your mind is purpose. Customers respond to the energy and enthusiasm that are created by a sense of purpose." But hang on a minute. That purpose can't be you. You must be other-focused, meaning you must understand the entire situation before you suggest or prescribe your product as the solution.

Say a person says they're starving, and you sell ultra-gluttonous, gluten-oozing Goo Goo Clusters and you immediately tell them, "Buy my product, you will love it and never feel starving again!" only to find out that person has gluten allergies, is diabetic, and hates clusters of any sort. Oops. You didn't even have a chance to explain that you offer a gluten-free, cluster-free, sugar-free option because you already put that person in the hospital with your presumptuous sales hastiness.

The right intent opens minds (and mouths), whereas the wrong intent closes them. The Eight Laws of Sales Intent are crucial to succeeding in our new world:

1. I intend to have empathy, to see things from the customer's point of view.
2. I intend to focus on them and not on me.
3. I intend to find people who truly want what I am offering.
4. I intend to be seen as different, unique, and the consummate professional.
5. I intend to master the knowledge I need to be seen as an expert in my business.
6. I intend to prepare for every call, not because it is important to me, but because it is important to my customers and prospects.
7. I intend to use words and find language that will resonate with my prospects and be compelling.
8. I intend to have an internal locus of control because I understand I am responsible for the outcomes of my actions.

In any conversation with a prospect, the first questions you ask can either make you or break you. They can either compel people to be drawn to you and become open to what you are selling, or they can completely turn them off to you and your products, triggering sales resistance that undoubtedly leads to the dreaded rejection.

If you want to ensure prospective clients become actual customers, keep reading. You're on the right track. The internet is littered with articles about the sales process and sales process tips. What makes this any different? Because we provide you with a *questioning* process that works *with* human behavior and not against it.

The truth is your sales may not be where you want them to be based on three simple concepts.

1. Your definition of sales
2. Your word choice
3. What you're *not* asking

That last one is the most critical and is interdependent on the other two. Now that you have a better understanding of sales and how your words matter, it's time to break down the questioning process.

Connection Questions

Connection questions are the key to creating a favorable first impression while focusing on your potential customer. Through them, you'll form an emotional connection with them that 99 percent of salespeople only can hope to have. Notice the dramatic difference in the tonality and flow and pick up on the three very powerful connection questions used right at the start of the sales conversation that immediately draws the prospect in like an HBO limited series whodunnit starring Nicole Kidman or Kate Winslet.

Being able to establish control in the conversation from the beginning empowers you to be open to your prospects, and as such, you can help guide the sales conversation to a logical conclusion for them. Using connection questions also helps you to establish value in *you* and the company you represent.

Once you have learned what connection questions are and why and when to use them, it will be easy to put the focus on your prospect and establish trust. Like a CBD-infused gummy bear, these questions, when used correctly, will eliminate the anxiety that dooms a sales pitch from the start.

Now let's see how to use a connection question to start the sales process when someone calls you after seeing an advertisement, this time, for an insurance company.

> **Prospect:** *"I'm calling about your ad I saw online. Could you tell me what it's all about?"*
>
> **New Model Salesperson:** *"Oh, for sure I can go through all the details with you if you'd like, but I was just curious when you went through the ad, what was it about it that attracted your attention?"*

This is your first connection question.

Why would you ask them this question? There are actually two reasons.

The first is because they'll tell you, but more importantly, they'll tell themselves why they were even interested in reaching out in the first place. This is the first step toward them persuading themselves to fully listen to you and what you have to offer. The second is that you'll now start to see a picture of why they called and what they need.

> **Prospect:** *"I was curious about . . . yadda, yadda, yadda . . ."*
>
> After they tell you why they responded to the ad, you then ask an additional connection question.
>
> **New Model Salesperson:** *"Was there anything* else *that attracted your attention?"* And there's your second connection question.

Many times, they will tell you more reasons why they responded to the ad. You're now getting a picture of their scenario, and it's starting to resemble a sale. Keep going.

> **New Model Salesperson:** *"Do you know what you're looking for?"* Your third connection question.

Then you can proceed with a situation question, depending on what you sell. This is how you might approach your first meeting with a prospect if you sold, say, life insurance.

> **New Model Salesperson:** *"Tell me, what type of life insurance policy do you have now?"* or *"Can I ask what type of financial coverage you have now for your family?"*

Here's how it might look when you first approach a doctor:

> **Prospect:** *"Nice to meet you. What company did she say you are with? OK, I'm in a bit of a hurry, what are you selling?"*
>
> **New Model Salesperson:** *"Nice to meet you as well. I'm wondering whether the reason we are meeting today is that you heard about our new chip for broken legs that are in casts and wanted to hear about it?"*
>
> **Prospect:** *"No, I have not heard about a product like you just described, but you have me curious, that's for sure."*
>
> **New Model Salesperson:** *"I take from your curiosity that now might be a good time to give you a quick overview of the DMW chip since you are busy. I just need to ask you two quick questions, so I don't waste your time. Is that OK? By the way, our company is called DMW, Inc. which stands for "Don't Make It Worse!""*

Now let's see how a salesperson who uses traditional selling techniques calls an outbound lead to sell coaching services using both the old-school and New Model methods.

> **Average Salesperson:** *"Hi, is this Annie? Annie, this is Lara Craft with XYZ Company. How are you doing today? Great. Hey, do you have two minutes to talk right now?"*
>
> **Prospect:** *"No, I really don't."*
>
> **Average Salesperson:** *"OK, well, I saw you responded to an ad yesterday about getting a coach to help you close more deals in business, and I've been asked to personally call you to show you how we can help you get more deals in your business. When works best to call you back? Later today or tomorrow?"*

You're starting to chase them, and now you look like what? Just another over-eager salesperson trying to sell them something.

> **Prospect:** *"Give me a call tomorrow."*

> **Average Salesperson:** *"OK, great! So, Annie, let me ask you a question really quick. What are two problems you're having right now that are costing you deals and money?"*
>
> **Prospect:** *"I'm doing really well in my business right now. What's this all about anyway?"*
>
> **Average Salesperson:** *"Well, I'm calling you because, with our coaching services, we can help you close more deals and help you with your business needs. In fact, we have been rated the number one coaching service in the country for three years in a row by our clients, and . . ."*
>
> **Prospect** [Cuts the salesperson off]: *"Well, I'm busy right now. Just call back tomorrow."*
>
> **Average Salesperson:** *"OK, well, let me ask you again what two problems you're having right now that are costing you deals and money, that if I could fix them for you right now, you would take me seriously and spend a few minutes with me."*

Notice how the salesperson keeps pushing for the prospect to tell her two problems. The sales pressure is mounting right now.

> **Prospect:** *"Look ma'am, I don't really have that many problems."*
>
> **Average Salesperson:** *"Then why did you respond to the ad? I have a solution that will help you follow up with your prospects to get your company so many deals that you could triple your sales this next month. When could you give me ten minutes where I could show you how this will work for your company?"*
>
> **Prospect:** *"Yeah, maybe next week sometime."*
>
> **Average Salesperson:** *"OK, I could do Thursday at two or Friday at one."*

This is known as the "trial close." Every salesperson uses this, and prospects feel that you're pressuring them for an appointment.

> **Prospect:** *"I could do Friday at one."*
>
> **Average Salesperson:** *"OK, great. I know you are really going to like what I am going to show you on Friday. I am so excited. Talk to you then."*

Then next Friday at one in the afternoon, the only thing the average salesperson hears is a voice mail message, so she leaves a message, but the prospect never calls her back. Shocker. Once again, water is also wet. Has this ever happened to you?

Now let's see how a New Model professional salesperson calls a lead to sell coaching services.

> **New Model Salesperson:** *"Hi, Jane, this is Jeff Lebowski. I am with XYZ Coaching Company, and it looks like you responded to an ad yesterday about possibly having outside help in scaling your coaching business. I should probably start off by asking, have you found what you are looking for, or are you still looking for help to scale your business?"*

Always ask, because if they have already found help, you would want to know that up front. Ninety-nine percent of the time, they will tell you that they haven't.

> **Prospect:** *"No, I'm still looking."*
> **New Model Salesperson:** *"OK, I was just curious what was it about the ad that attracted your attention?"*

This reminds them why they responded to the ad. Notice how they are not only telling you why they responded but more importantly who are they telling? They are telling *themselves*. This is how you'll get them to persuade themselves to want to look at how you might be able to help them.

Now we set the frame of the call.

> **New Model Salesperson:** *"This first part of the call I would say is more for us to find out more about what you've done in the past to scale, and really what you're looking for now, just to see if we could actually help you, as there are just some people out there that there's not much we can do for them."*

Now, why would I say this at the end here? It's because it *disarms* the prospect. When you say you're not sure whether you can even help them yet, as there are some people/companies who you *cannot* help, it triggers their brain to start to pull you in.

Remember to listen *carefully* to the answer and take notes.

New Model Salesperson: *"And do you know what you're looking for?"*

Or:

"And what were you hoping to get out of the call today, just so I understand better?"

Whether you call leads, go B2B, cold call, or network, it's imperative that you focus on the potential customer instead of on your own agenda. In this situation, your agenda is their agenda, so by focusing on them, you'll be able to find out what they want and why they want it from the very beginning.

Now it's time to take it to the next level, a deeper level in which you will ask the DNA of the sales conversation known as *situation questions*, the foundation on which you'll build your *entire* sales conversation.

Situation Questions

To get to the end goal, we must first learn what a potential customer's present situation is, what problems they're having, the cause of those problems, and how said problems are affecting them (what emotion are they feeling). This must be done *before* we can offer our solution to see whether we can even help them. We can't change what the customer thinks unless we know what they think and how they approach a situation where our product or service might be the right solution.

Your potential customers have the answers. They are the hosts of this game show—the Alex Trebek (RIP), Mayim Bialik, Ken Jennings (and whoever else *Jeopardy!* chose by the time you get to this chapter) of your tournament of sales champs. All you need to do to win is to simply ask the right questions and give them time to answer. You'll take Winning Sales Strategies for a thousand before they have time to go to commercial break.

Let's have a look at how to call someone who has requested to have information sent to them. We'll see how the New Model Salesperson calls a prospect who has been sent information about a company or obtained information from the company's website.

Most salespeople would make this call assuming that the prospect intends to make a purchase simply because they requested information be sent to them. But you know better than that. You're going to remain calm, collected, and neutral to find out whether you can help this person.

> **New Model Salesperson:** *"Hi Mary, this is Charles Kane from XYZ Company. You recently asked us to send you information regarding our digital marketing strategies for small business owners, and I was calling you back to see whether we could possibly help you. Is this an appropriate time?"*
>
> **Prospect:** *"Yes, this is fine. I have a few minutes."*
>
> **New Model Salesperson:** *"I should probably start out by asking you, have you found what you are looking for, or are you still looking for ways to get more qualified leads?"*

Notice how, at the end of the sentence, we plugged in what, specifically, they responded to the ad for (in this case, getting more quality leads)? You just plug the benefit in at the end and boom!

There's your first connection question. This immediately opens up the conversation like a corkscrew. Pop! Now it's time to let the wine breathe. Your question is to make sure they haven't already found something else or signed a contract with someone else because if they have and did, it's game over and no one's time has been wasted. That being said, since they just responded to the ad, 99 percent of the time it means they are still looking.

> **New Model Salesperson:** *"OK, I was just curious, when you went through the ad where you saw XYZ, what was it about the ad that attracted your attention?"*

This is your second connection question. This reminds them of why they responded to the ad in the first place and, in addition to telling you, who are they telling? They are telling themselves! This is the first part of them persuading themselves to want to let you help them. Remember, this is not *Jerry Maguire* and "Help me help you." This is you helping them to help themselves. You follow?

> **Prospect:** *"Well, I guess I was just curious about what you guys do. We have a company now that helps us with this kind of stuff, so I was just more curious than anything else."*
>
> **New Model Salesperson:** *"That's not a problem."*

This is a simple way to defuse the objection of already having a company.

> **New Model Salesperson:** *"Yes, I can go through a few details if you'd like. It might be appropriate if I knew a little bit more about your company and what you do to see whether we could actually help you in the first place. For example, what type of marketing do you use to bring in new leads and clients?"*

This New Model Salesperson is asking a few situation questions to get a picture of what they do to determine whether or not they have problems that the salesperson's solution can address and solve.

> **Prospect:** *"We actually do some PPC, banner ads, and some Facebook ads."*
>
> **New Model Salesperson:** *"How long have you been doing that type of marketing?"*

They're now full throttle in a two-way conversation with the prospect and involving them in the process. They're not that dreaded salesperson who's just trying to sell them something.

Now that you've seen some examples and we've discussed why it's so important to create a dialogue, here's a quick summary of the steps to take when calling your leads.

1. State who you are.
2. State where you are from.
3. Reference the ad they responded to and remind them that they asked you to call them.
4. Ask them whether this is still an appropriate time.

5. Indicate that you are not biased by stating the obvious: *"Our product (or service) is not for everyone. That's not the question. The question is who might benefit from what our product or service offers that you may not be thinking about now. Does it makes sense for us to continue the conversation to see if (what we do) can actually help you?*

6. Find out what their present situation is and, using connection and situation questions, ask how you can potentially help them.

What emotions do you think are most often aroused for both you and your potential customer during the start of a sales conversation? Anxiety and fear are most often associated with selling.

Connection questions enable you to put the focus on your prospect and establish trust, as they evaporate anxiety and fear effortlessly. You will no longer have to wonder what to say, and you won't have to find something of common interest to discuss. Small talk is excruciating and a reason why people these days text message more than they speak on the actual phone. Cut to the chase and cue the celebratory emojis!

Now let's move on to the situation part of the sales conversation. Your goal is to focus on a powerful common *bond*. This is when you show them that your interests are in alignment with theirs because you care about what they care about. What do you think their number one interest is? Obviously, their interest is themselves, their *situation*, and how said situation is affecting them, a.k.a. their problem(s).

Asking these questions empowers you to feel comfortable and confident in what you are selling. Your prospects can feel your confidence, and they'll feel comfortable with you. Remember, when you focus on your prospect, it will decrease your anxiety. These questions will also set the stage for you to continue asking them your skilled questions throughout the sales conversation. By knowing when to ask specific questions, you'll know what to listen for and you'll know when and how to present your solution.

They will question why they allow themselves to stay in that same situation. Then, they will start to think about doing something to change their situation. When your potential clients get to this point, because of your questioning skills, they will start to persuade themselves on being ready to make that change now, not in six months or a year, but *now*.

The questions you ask create more problems in their mind, issues they didn't even know they had, bringing them to the point where they're ready to hear how you may be able to help solve those issues, saying, "Oh, I didn't even think we had these issues. We have to solve these because here's where I will be if we get them solved. But if not, I'm going to stay right where I currently am."

As a general rule of thumb, you don't want to ask more than three to four situation questions in a row. If you ask more than that, your prospects may feel that you are interrogating them like a cop on a *Dateline* episode. Difference here is, they're free to go. And you don't want that. While situation questions tend to be boring and devoid of emotion, they're still very necessary.

They help you to learn what their present situation is, what they are doing right now, and what they've done in the past. The answers you receive will be more factual than anything else.

Situation questions can be used in any industry regardless of what you sell. Here are some examples:

Network Marketing

In network marketing, your goal is most likely to recruit people to join your sales organization. Here are a few questions you could ask: *"So, John, what do you do for a living?"* or *"What do you do for work?"* Then you would ask, *"How long have you been doing that type of work?"* or *"How long have you been doing that for a living?"*

If your prospect is a business owner, you could ask, *"How long have you owned that type of business?"*

If your prospect is retired, you could ask, *"How long have you been retired? What did you do before you retired?"*

Then you could ask one more situation question: *"So what got you involved in your career?"* or *"What got you involved in that type of work?"*

Financial Services

Suppose your prospect is a high-net-worth individual. You can ask, *"May I ask, what does your investment portfolio look like now?"* *"And how long have you been allocating your principal into those types of investments?"* and *"I am curious what got you involved in that type of investing?"*

Car Sales

"So tell me, Julie, what type of car do you drive now?" "And how long have you had your vehicle?" and *"I'm curious what caused you to purchase that car a few years ago?"*

Life Insurance Sales

"So can I ask who you use for your life insurance now?" "And what type of policy do you have with that company?" "I'm curious what caused you to choose that company/ policy?" "What do you have in place now to financially protect your family when you do pass away?" "OK, and how long have you been with that company?" or *"Can I ask what caused you to use that company over someone else?"*

B2B Medical Sales

Jerry has his own spin on how to approach doctors if you are in the B2B medical field dealing with doctors. Check this out:

> **New Model Salesperson:** *"So can I ask you this? I know every practice is different but, in your practice, do you find yourself seeing more patients with broken legs in a boot than you would like to see, that have to be counseled, maybe harshly, by your staff about keeping that boot on as instructed or risk the consequences of really messing up that broken leg?*
>
> *"I'm curious, Dr., how big a problem for these patients can it potentially be in your experience to be that noncompliant with such an injury?*
>
> *"If you had to guess about how many times in a month might a patient like that be seen in your office?*
>
> *"Dr., since this kind of challenge can have a very negative impact on a patient's recovery, how do you typically approach this challenge with patients you feel are not being compliant with your recommendations about wearing their boot?"*

See how this works? It's far from exciting, but it's fairly straightforward. You're getting an idea of their present situation to understand where they are coming from before you move on to finding out why they could possibly want to make a change.

Choosing to always focus on your prospect will give you that competitive edge. And we don't mean asking about their personal life, how many kids they have, etc. We mean focusing on finding out what their business problems are, what caused those problems, and how they're affecting them.

Connection questions enable you to put the focus on your prospect and establish trust, as they evaporate anxiety and fear effortlessly. That leads us straight into the next step in the power of dialogue. You ready? Things are about to get serious here. We're getting engaged!

In the next chapter, we will be diving further into the engagement stage with problem awareness, solution awareness, and consequence, qualifying, probing, and clarifying questions so you are one step closer to the commitment stage. And unlike your stubborn, still-single fraternity brother from thirty years ago, even the biggest commitment-phobes have been known to cave to New Model maneuvers.

Chapter 9

The Engagement Stage

Customers don't care about your policies. =
Find and engage the need. Tell the customer what you can do.
—Alice Sesay Pope, customer experience motivational speaker

More than ever before, we salespeople must engage our prospects as individual people—as human beings, not numbers—before we can move forward with our solutions. This is true in our sales conversations with potential customers, and now it is equally true at a macro level in our advertising and marketing efforts.

The engagement stage is the core of the NEPQ-based New Model of Selling. This is where the sale is made in the sales process. It's 85 percent of the process. You will notice that your customers will buy *you* (this is totally different from "being bought," BTW), first based on your listening, being understanding, and then asking them the right questions at the right time in your conversation.

Your goal is to help them find out what their problems are, if any, what caused those problems, specifically the root cause, and most importantly, how these problems are affecting them and/or their own customers. And, as you now know, you find all that out by asking questions. Now that you're engaged, it's time to pry into your prospect's deepest, darkest *business* demons—strategically, of course.

Problem Awareness Questions

Asking problem awareness questions helps you and your prospect explore what their challenges are and how those problems are impacting them.

When they answer these questions, it'll be like having your very own sales Waze, with a detailed road map of how they got to the situation they are in, as well as the bumps, speed traps, and accidents along the way. You'll understand what their problems are, why they have those problems, and what those problems are doing to them.

When do you ask them? Right after you ask them two to three situation questions, you will then start asking them problem awareness questions. Always start out by asking them whether they like what they have now. Of course, this will be phrased slightly differently in a B2B sale in which, say, a tire manufacturer is selling tires to a car manufacturer or wholesalers selling their products to retailers, but you'll get the idea with the following examples.

> **Car sales:** *"So, John, do you like the car you have now?"*
> **Life insurance:** *"So, Mary, do you like the insurance policy you have now?"*
> **Real Estate:** *"So, Alex, do you like your home you live in now?"*
> **Network marketing/Recruiting agency:** *"So, Jane, do you like what you're doing for a living now?"*
> **Financial services:** *"So, Barry, do you like your portfolio you have now?"*
> **Weight loss services:** *"So, Drew, do you like the diet programs you use now?"*
> **Medical:** *"So, Dr., do you like the way that patients with broken legs are able to make the decision to not wear their boot as they should without you knowing in real time?"*

Or it could be worded this way: *"Do you want your patients to be able to take their boot off without you knowing?"* and when they come back and say, *"Heck, no,"* you would ask them an NEPQ probing question such as, *"But why though?"* or *"Why is it so important for you to know whether they are taking off the boot or not?"*

Do you see how this works? You're just asking to see whether they like what they have now, what they're using now, or what they're doing now. There is no right or wrong answer here. Whether they say that they do or don't like what they already have, simply follow the path they lead you on with their answers to your questions.

It's also equally important to find out what they *do* like about their current provider, service, product, or occupation because you will need to know what's important to them about their service or what they are using now so that you'll know whether your solution can also give them that as well.

On the flip side, if your sales conversation starts going down a path where they don't like what they are currently using or have, then you will explore what they don't like about it and why, and how it's affecting them. Most importantly, be neutral here with your questions. Always show interest in both sides of what they already like and what they don't like.

The benefits of problem awareness questions are plenty.

1. They encourage your prospective customers to share their opinions, emotions, feelings, and worries. They feel safe with you, trust you, and feel they can open up.

2. They encourage your prospects to share their likes and dislikes and how their problems are affecting them.

3. They give both of you a front-row seat to what their problems are, what caused those problems, and why it's important for them to change.

4. They make you look extremely smart, professional, and considerate. You'll become a trusted expert, and you'll also become *the* trusted authority in your prospect's mind. Plus, you'll form a priceless emotional connection that can't be bought with free, two-day shipping on Amazon Prime.

5. While most salespeople only get the facts, you'll be getting their emotions and feelings. You'll get everything and then some. You are a New Model boss.

Turning Your Statements into Questions

Pro tip: instead of *making* statements, compose your statements into questions.

When it comes to today's information-overloaded buyer, turning your statements into questions is absolutely essential. When you're faced with a prospect who has a concern, don't jump to treat the concern like an objection. Instead, address their concerns by asking questions to fully understand their concern and help them sell themselves on the change they need to make.

Turning your statements into questions is easy, and it allows your prospects to become open to your ideas while simultaneously helping them overcome their own concerns. Consider it a form of multitasking if you will.

So how is this done? First, let's not confuse this with what *Psychology Today* calls "uptalk," in which people end their statements with inflections that sound like questions but aren't remotely questions (find a YouTube video of a Kardashian to see what we mean here). What we're talking about here is using statements like, "What if," "What do you think about," "Do you think," and "If you could."

By doing this, you'll be able to make suggestions but with a question. For example, *"What if it wasn't what you thought it was? Would you be open to looking at it from another perspective?"* or *"What if you could know instantly whether a patient with a serious broken leg has not worn their boot in a few days? Would you want to see how that can now be a possibility?"*

Another pro tip: remember *not* to tell your potential customers about what you know and what you have. Instead, ask questions that will uncover and explore what *they* know about the subject first.

If you show your cards right away, you're likely to lose. Same goes for immediately revealing your solution to your prospects. If you do, you may be the one who ends up owning the problem and the solution. This would mean that your potential prospect would be far less attached because they weren't involved in the process. This approach is far less persuasive.

Just watch what happens when your prospects start listening to themselves answering your questions. They'll start to process the information internally as they are talking. Their answers will help them think about their problems and to *own* the notion that they want to change those problems.

As they consciously and subconsciously internalize what they are saying to you, their answers will help them examine and challenge their own beliefs to learn why they keep allowing their present situation to continue.

When you ask these questions and people tell you their problems, why they have those problems, what's causing those problems, and how important it is for them to change their problems, they'll start thinking to themselves:

"Why do I keep putting off buying life insurance for my family?"

"Why do I keep investing my money with this firm?"

"Maybe I should look at what this lady is going over with me . . . maybe I could get a higher return?"

"Man, why do I keep commuting to work an hour each way when I could be like this guy working from home?"

"Wow, why do I keep advertising my business this way when I could be getting leads that have higher conversions for my sales team?"

There are countless examples, but the bottom line is that prospects will keep questioning themselves, asking, *"What's preventing me from doing this?"* or *"What's holding me back?"* They will question why they allow themselves to stay in the same situation and then, woot woot, they will start to think about *doing* something to change their situation.

When your potential clients reach this point because of *your* questioning skills, they will start to persuade themselves that they are ready to make that change today. You just leveled up and got them where you and they want to be. Congratulations!

If your potential client convinces themselves based on your questions to buy that nice, expensive red car, do you think that's more powerful than you telling them the reasons why they should buy that car? Insert water/wet joke here. Hello! Since the motivation is not external, the decision will feel natural to your prospect and that it's their idea to buy.

A Tale of Two Truths

What happens when your prospect tells you they love the company, product, or service they are already using? You probably feel instantly deflated because you were hoping for an all-out rant on how they hate it, it sucks, it's worse than gas station sushi, something like that. But don't fret.

The good news is that it doesn't matter if they are in love with what they already have because most people have two truths, in that very few people love or hate 100 percent of what they have or use. There is always something they don't like or something they'd like to improve. So are we saying everyone has an inner

Karen in them, with tendencies to complain about things? Nah. Because instead of asking for the manager, your prospects will just ask you for a solution.

If your potential customer says they like their current provider, the way for you to diffuse that is to ask, *"It sounds like things are going fairly well for you. Is there anything you would change about the results you're getting if you could?"*

Or you could reword it this way if you were selling in a more complex selling environment: *"So back when you chose to work with that company* (current vendor), *what were your selection criteria if I could ask?"*

Let *them* tell you. Then ask this question: *"In what ways has that possibly changed* (criteria) *as you look at your needs today though?"* This question allows you to see and understand why their current situation is different from what it was when they started working with the other vendor. It opens the door for you to clarify and probe and help them find problems they didn't think they had.

That's the formula to uncover the *real* truth. Just tailor it to what you sell.

If you ask this question at the right time, they will contradict what they just told you. The New Model Salesperson knows that the first answer will usually reflect their "protected history," but the second answer reveals what they would *want* to happen. And you're here to help make that happen.

Let's look at an example of how the Average Salesperson and the New Model Salesperson respond when the potential customer says they love their current provider and are happy with the service they are getting.

> **Prospect:** *"Well, we really like our current provider. We have very good premiums, and our coverage is excellent."*
>
> **Average Salesperson:** *"Well, I know how you feel. Others I have talked to have felt the same way when I first met them, but they found that they could get better insurance through my company."*

Using the old sales technique, the "feel, felt, found" with today's consumer doesn't work anymore. It's worn out; it's *so* twentieth century. Your prospects have had it used on them by every other salesperson trying to sell them something, so it automatically triggers sales pressure and resistance. They're over it, and they think you're just like the rest of them. Prove them wrong by learning what *not* to do.

Average Salesperson: *"If I could show you how my company's insurance is better than your provider now, wouldn't it make sense for you to switch over?"*

The phrase, "If I could show you" puts the pressure on you to prove that yours is better and the potential customer will feel sales pressure when you say this. The funny thing is that the salesperson can also feel that same sales pressure as well and it's awkward.

Prospect: *"Well, my wife will be home tonight, and I can talk to her about what you're offering and call you back later this week. Why don't you leave a brochure and I'll call you back if she's interested?"*

Average Salesperson: *"Well . . . wouldn't she want your family to have a better insurance rate? I'll tell you what, let me call my manager and see if he would be willing to lower the cost a bit for you. If I got it lowered a bit, could you make a decision now? Because after today, our promotion ends for the rest of the year."*

Do you really think the "let me talk to my manager" routine works anymore in the post-trust era? These days, only the aforementioned kvetchy Karens talk to managers and both you and your potential client know that. Do you think they'll also feel the sales pressure that salespeople put on them? They do! Then what happens next? They get turned off, shut the door, hang up the phone, or leave the meeting. Whatever the situation, the sale is lost.

Prospect: *"Like I said, I need to talk to my wife about it first. Have a great night."* Click! The prospect hangs up the phone. Bye, Felicia; bye, Karen; bye, sale.

Now here's how the New Model Salesperson responds to a prospect who's happy with their current product/service:

Prospect: *"Well, we really like our current service provider. They've done an amazing job for us."*

New Model Salesperson: *"That's not a problem. Just curious what do you like about them?"*

Prospect: *"We like how they . . ."*

New Model Salesperson: *"Anything else you like about them?"*

Prospect: *"Yes, they really do a good job with . . ."*

New Model Salesperson: *"So to me, it sounds like things are going fairly well for you. Is there anything you would change about your provider and financial coverage if you could?"*

You'll find that 99 percent of the time when you ask this question at the right time in the conversation, they will tell you something completely different from what they said at first. You'll learn what they don't like and what they want changed.

Now in this example, let's say you sell some type of widget to companies in a more B2B complex selling environment, and you've asked the two truths questions. Watch how they reply:

Prospect: *"Well, we like them. But lately, we have noticed that they are increasing their monthly cost by about 12 percent, and it has some of us concerned."*

New Model Salesperson: *"What do you mean by concerned?"*

Prospect: *"Well, you know, we are trying to cut our costs around here."*

New Model Salesperson: *"Is there anything else you would change about what they do for you if you could?"*

Prospect: *"Well, another thing is, they seem to be much slower with all the supply chain issues, and we don't hear back from them sometimes for days."*

Can you see how there are two truths? They just told you a few things they don't like and would want to change. This could be the tipping point for your prospect. Now you will continue asking them questions about the issues they are having, why they are having them, how these issues are affecting them and their company, and how important is it for them to change their situation. Hang in there, you're en route to sales greatness.

Probing, Consequence & Clarifying Questions

Once your prospective customer reveals their problem(s) to you, asking them probing, consequence, and clarifying questions makes it easy for your prospect to relive their experience of what the problem has done to them. It allows them to develop the story in very painful detail. And while you don't want to trigger PTSD in them, you do want them to become keenly aware of how much of a problem (or problems) they really do have.

Probing Questions

Your probing questions invite your prospect to elaborate and bring out their emotions and feelings. Without asking probing questions at the right time, you don't bring out the emotions of your prospect, so they don't feel they need to change.

Here are some good questions to ask:

> *"How long has that been going on for?*
> *"Has that had an impact on you?"*
> *"In what way?"*
> *"What bothers you the most about this?"*
> *"How tough a position did that put you in?"*

What's great about probing questions, which are crucial at this point in the conversation, is that they don't intrude on the prospect's privacy because they're the ones who are opening up to you as a trusted confidant or adviser.

Pro tip: not every probe has to be in the form of a question. This is not *Jeopardy!* (who's the host now?). You can try a comment like, *"I sense you may be frustrated by this* [insert problem here]." Use whatever invites your prospect to express their frustrations and bring out their feelings. That's all you need to do.

Clarifying Questions

Clarifying questions allow you and your prospect to go much deeper than they would normally go with a typical salesperson. This is next-level sales. As you use these questions, you will find that there is an aura of intensity surrounding their need. Some of the problems you'll uncover based on the answers to your questions don't just call for satisfaction, they *demand* satisfaction. This need will now become attached to your prospect. They'll own their problems. Now you're both connected and determined to solve their problems. You're in it. Let's do this.

Here are a few examples of clarifying questions:

"Can I ask why you said that?"
"What do you mean by that?"
"How do you mean?"
"When you say that . . . what do you mean exactly?"
"How do you feel about that?"
"Can I ask you why you want that though?"

It's important to realize that when you get answers to your first questions, most of the time these will be just surface answers. They're not the real answers. So, if you just accept their answers and move on, then you are missing what is really going on. This is a huge reason why you are losing a lot of sales that you could be making because you are not going deeper than the surface with your questions. New Model Salespeople dig so deep they find layers their prospects never even knew existed. They may even find Jimmy Hoffa in their digging expeditions, that's how deep they go.

Once you have mastered this skill, you have risen to the highest financial status in your sales career. If that's not an incentive, we don't know what is.

Here are more questions to bring out their emotions and to peel more layers of the onion.

"Can you tell me more about . . ."
"Could you elaborate more on that?"
"I'm not sure I understand . . ."
"How does your spouse/boss feel about that?"
"Why do you say that?"
"Why now though?"
"Is there anything else I should know about that?"

"Why do you feel that way still?"
"So what you're saying is . . . ?"
"Can you help me better understand . . . ?"

A prospect might reply with: *"There's a lot on the line here . . ."* or *"I've been stuck with this situation."* And you could respond with a clarifying question like *"In what way?"* or *"What do you mean by stuck?"*

Here's a dialogue between a salesperson who's in charge of conventions at a resort and a prospective customer who wants to select the right resort for their company's annual convention:

> **Prospect:** *"In the past, with the resorts we have used, we've had problems with check-ins and our dinner service."*
>
> **New Model Salesperson:** *"How do you mean, exactly?"*
>
> **Prospect:** *"It's really just the timing. I cannot fly all of our employees in between 2:30 p.m. and 5:00 p.m. for check-in so they can be ready for the welcome reception by 6:30 p.m. We really have to have some rooms ready by noon or 1:00 p.m. The employees get upset when they get to the check-in counter and their rooms are not ready."*
>
> **New Model Salesperson:** *"Can you tell me how this affects you when it happens?"*
>
> **Prospect:** *"Well, everyone starts calling me, then my boss jumps me. It happened a few months ago, and I thought I might lose my job."*
>
> **New Model Salesperson:** *"How did that make you feel?"*
>
> **Prospect:** *"Devastated, to say the least. I have a family to take care of, so I can't lose my job."*
>
> **New Model Salesperson:** *"So this is important to you to get it right?"*
>
> **Prospect:** *"Oh, you have no idea."*
>
> **New Model Salesperson:** *"You had also mentioned you were concerned about the dinner service. Can you tell me more about that?"*
>
> **Prospect:** *"We usually have over five hundred people at the welcome reception. Usually, the last eight to ten tables get served cold food. It causes those tables to get really upset."*
>
> **New Model Salesperson:** *"Does it have an impact on you when that happens?"*

> **Prospect:** *"Yes it does. I then have to go in crisis mode and help calm them down when I should be directing my attention to the after-dinner event."*
>
> **New Model Salesperson:** *"That makes sense. Tell me, what other points of concern do you have?"*
>
> **Prospect:** *"I don't really have any other concerns. We just need to make sure it's well planned out and then executed."*
>
> **New Model Salesperson:** *"I can show you how our hotel operations can be tailored to your schedule if you'd like. Would that possibly take some pressure off you?"*
>
> **Prospect:** *"Wow, it sure would. When can we do that?"*

Boom. You just made the sale, even though other resorts could meet this prospect's needs. Here's why. The facts about this prospect's needs have been heard by every hotel salesperson with whom this customer has spoken. And we all know that every salesperson says that they can meet those needs and that the concerns will not happen with their resort, right? Every salesperson has promised that. So the prospect has become skeptical because they've heard this promise many times.

However, the feelings and emotions about this prospect's needs have only been heard by you, the New Model Salesperson. Do your prospects make buying decisions based on logic (facts) or emotions (feelings)? We know they base them on emotion and will justify with logic.

In the resort case, the salesperson heard the facts around the prospect's problems and was in no hurry to jump in with an insta-solution. The New Model Salesperson listens and asks purposeful probing questions to uncover the emotional side of this prospect.

Solution Awareness Questions

Once you've asked the appropriate problem awareness, probing, and clarifying questions, you will have demonstrated to your potential customer that you are the antithesis of other salespeople. You are a sales excavator as opposed to your competitors, who barely scrape the surface. Now that you're a trusted authority in your prospects' eyes, it's time to go full-blown Sherlock on them and try to figure out exactly what your potential customers understand about what they are looking for.

Obviously, they know their own story better than anyone. They'll know how things are in their world and how they got to that point. However, they may not fully understand how your product or service fits into that picture of their world, and they may not yet know how to connect the past and the future together.

You'll need to help your prospect create a picture of their past and their present situation. In 1902, Journalist and *Jungle Book* author Rudyard Kipling wrote, "I keep six honest serving-men (they taught me all I knew); Their names are What and Why and When, and How and Where and Who." Kipling believed that the answers he received from his six questions gave him workable stories. This guy won the Nobel Prize for Literature and has a Guinness World Record for still, today, being the youngest to win it at forty-two. Not too shabby. But back to those questions.

Those same questions can be used today with your prospects to find out what they have done about changing their situation, and more importantly, to discover how they would feel about solving their problems and moving forward. The answers they give you will help them consciously and subconsciously see, that by taking action, they can indeed change their situation and solve their problems. They will start to feel the benefits of having their situation changed as they listen to their own words. We call this their *objective state*. What their future will look like once these problems that your questions have helped them see they have, are ultimately solved and they get what they want. Amazing, isn't it? You, too, will revel in this self-discovery! But don't put the champagne on ice just yet.

This is the power that is behind the solution awareness questions you ask. These questions help your prospect come up with the solution themselves as opposed to having you tell them what the solution is. There will be a place for you to bring up your solution and how you can help during the presentation stage of the process, but not yet.

Salespeople who use traditional selling techniques feel that because they have all the knowledge about their product or service, they have to prove that to their prospect quickly to appear smart. Not so fast.

Your excitement about telling your prospect what you know too soon in the conversation will keep you from discovering what your prospect actually knows. Premature revelation is a rookie move. The key is to use your ability to ask skilled questions, not to tell your prospects what you know. Telling is not selling. Set those lyrics to Auto-Tune. Never let your need to tell stand in the way of allowing your prospect to give you the answers about what they are looking for.

You can actually ask solution awareness questions at any time during your sales conversation. They come in different forms and can be used in different situations.

Here are the two basic versions:

1. "What have you done about changing your situation?"
2. "What would you do if you could?"

Realize that many of your prospects are looking for ways to solve their problems. They might have explored different ways to do that but came up empty or tried other things and didn't succeed in solving their need(s).

The way for you to find out what they have done, if anything, is to ask variations of the following question:

"Have you been out there looking for anything that would give you what you're wanting?"

All you do is plug in what they have told you they are looking for and what results they want. In this example, we'll say that you sell financial services.

"John, before we talked today, were you out there looking for different investments that would give you a higher return than what you're currently getting?" or *"What were you doing about trying to find something to get you a higher rate of return?"*

In this next example, you sell business franchises, and Amy has already told you she wants to have a business where she can make more than her job.

"Amy, before you found us here at XYZ Franchise, were you out there looking for a business where you could start to make more money than you do with your job?" or *"What were you doing about finding your own business?"*

You could also ask the following:

"What have you done about changing this, if anything?"

In another example, we'll say that you sell insurance, and your prospect is Stuart, who has an existing policy. Based on the questions you asked him previously, you discovered that his wife was putting pressure on him to increase his policy's value. You found by going deeper in the conversation that when she was a child, her dad passed away and left her and her mom with very little money, and because of that she has a deep fear it could happen again. So you ask the following question:

"So, Stuart, what have you done in the past about getting more coverage that would give your family more financial protection when something does happen to you?

If your prospect tells you they have tried to solve their problems in the past or are out there looking for solutions now, ask them to expand on that. You *must* go deeper if you want to be at the top of your sales industry.

When you ask them what they have done about changing their situation in the past, ask them how they got involved with that company, product, etc., what worked, what didn't work, what they would have changed if they could have, what criteria they would use, and whether they'd like to do something else or do business with someone else.

Pro tip: in the post-trust era, since your customers are more skeptical than ever, they may even fear that once they transfer their money to you for your solution, you might let them down. They will ask themselves, "What if this product or service doesn't solve my problem?" If that happens, immediately interject what we call "pretend questions" to provoke the potential customer to make smaller decisions that move them forward in the buying process.

Here's the evolution of a pretend question:

"How do you see your life being different than it is now?"

This is a generic question, and we will just plug in what they told you they want changed, and you're going to ask them, *"How would it be different for you by making that change?"* and then, *"How would that make you feel?"*

The skilled questions you are learning will remove pressure from your potential customer and make them feel comfortable with you. It is much easier for your prospect to answer your question in a way that is just a "let's pretend, for a moment" type of question. Meaning, what you answer now doesn't really count; it's only seeing with your imagination. It's just pretend. As Mr. Rogers said, "Pretending doesn't require expensive toys." Just be sure to pretend by applying these three rules to your conversation:

Pretend Rule #1: Use Conditional Language

Make the decision conditional. Your question could be something like, *"If you were to go ahead with this, when would you do that?"* Meaning, just for a moment, pretend, imagine you're going ahead with a final decision. The front end of that question is what's called a "lead-in." The last part of the question will bring out a specific decision, such as:

> *"If you were to go ahead with . . . when would you . . . ?"*
> *"Where would you . . . ?"*
> *"What kind would you . . . ?"*
> *"How many would you . . . ?"*

The great part about pretend questions is that they are very easy to answer. Why? Because they don't pressure or pose any risk to your prospect.

Pretend Rule #2: Remove the Salesperson

Nicely, of course, not in a *Sopranos* kind of way.

You must leave out the word "I" and focus on them and their world. Reduce your prospect's sense of risk by using neutral language.

Here is how *not* to do it: *"If I could get you to agree that my investment opportunity is a good idea . . ."* or *"When could I get you to sign the contract?"*

Using "I" and "my" tells your potential customer that you're self-absorbed and not there for them, likely causing them to get defensive and downright done with you.

Try something like this: *"If there was a way that we could help you get a much higher rate of return than what you currently have, is that something you might be looking for?"*

Pretend Rule #3: Remove the Company and Product Name

Do not assume the potential customer has decided to buy yet. Therefore, always exclude your company's name and your product's or service's name from the question. Keep your question very neutral.

Again, here is how *not* to do it:

"If you go with our XYZ Internet Service Program . . ."

When you ask your prospect to make a conditional decision and you attach the name of your company or brand name, it comes across to your customer like you're assuming that they will make a purchase. That's too presumptuous. Your company name creates sales pressure especially if the customer is already using another company's service/product, so just leave it out. Try something like this:

"If you were to start a new internet service program . . ."

Consequence Questions

So, you probed, you clarified, you scored (as in you helped them discover a problem, or better yet, *multiple* problems), and now your goal is to get the prospect to reveal what will happen if they do nothing about the newly revealed problem. This is where you use the question, *"What if?"*

> *"What if you don't do anything about this problem, and your situation gets even worse?"*
> *"What if the product or service you're thinking of doesn't get you the results you want?"*

You're simply taking a problem that they themselves have told you they have and want to solve, and you'll ask them a question around that problem that allows them to think about the possible consequences of not doing anything to solve that problem.

Note: Average Salespeople like to use the customer's problems in a manipulative way to bully the customer into buying a product or service. New Model Salespeople do not tolerate bullying. Your goal is not to force anything, but rather, to empower the customer to realize that they themselves have the power to change their own situation.

Consequence questions can be structured into two formats.

1. Ask a question that gets them to think about problems they may not even know they have. Sometimes, experience in your industry from customers you have already helped allows you to see problems they might not see. For example, let's say one of your existing clients is thinking about leaving your company and going with a competitor. You could ask them something like this:

   "Have you considered what could happen if switching to a different company doesn't get you the results you said you want?"

   Then you could continue with something like this:

   "If there was a way we could get you the same results you want without you having to do all the work of changing companies, would you be open to looking at that as a possibility?"

   Next, sit back and let *them* reflect and respond on their decision to open a conversation that will allow you to show them how you could possibly help them get what they told you they want.

2. Ask these questions right after you ask a few solution awareness questions, which we go into more depth on below. Your goal is to get them to envision what will happen if they don't take any proactive action. Consequence questions will help create urgency to do something about their situation ASAP.

Here are a few examples of this format:

"Have you considered the possible ramifications of not doing anything about your situation?"
"Have you thought about what would happen if you don't do anything about this?"

A five-star consequence question, because it's the most powerful, is to ask, *"What happens if you don't do anything about this and you keep doing the same thing for the next three, six, or even twelve months?"* or depending on the industry, you may add at the end, *"five, ten, fifteen plus years"* to emphasize the longevity of their issues.

Here's a cheat sheet of more killer consequence questions:

"What would it do to you if you were not able to get what you're looking for?"
"What if it didn't work out for you?"
"What would happen if you didn't do anything about this?"
"Does that cause you to be concerned?"
"Have you considered the consequences of not doing anything?"
"What if you lost . . . ?"
"What would it do to you personally if you didn't solve this problem?"
"How would your life be different than it is now?"
"What would happen if you didn't get what you are looking for?"
"How would it make you feel if you were not able to solve this?"

Ask what it is they are looking for. What do they want—what kinds of products, services, features, applications, etc.?

Ask how many or how much do they want. Quantify the need for the product or service.

Ask when the product or service is going to be used, meaning a date for start-up preparations, date of delivery, date of implementation, or a date on a signed agreement.

Ask how long or how often is the product or service going to be used. Frequency, duration, time frame, etc.

Ask who is involved in making the decision, in using the product or service. Ask where is the product or service going to be delivered to or actually used. Does location enter into the conversation?

Qualifying Questions

Readers of a certain generation (X) will recall the race car video game *Pole Position*, which opened every race with the words, "Prepare to qualify." While this isn't a race, this is the part where you qualify your prospects in three main areas of the conversation:

1. At the beginning of the sales conversation (if you pick up on clues that they might not have funds to do business with you)
2. During the sales conversation
3. Before you present your solution

Your qualifying questions help people commit. Many of these questions will subliminally qualify them. Many of their answers will let you know they are qualified already. The qualification process is actually more important for your prospects than it is for you because it reinforces and imprints in their mind the decision to change their situation with you.

Remember, you're the facilitator who is taking them through this journey.

Fact: Most salespeople waste time by *not* qualifying their prospects. However, there is a fine line of tact that you need to adopt because if you go too heavy on the qualifying process, you'll end up turning off many of your prospects.

If, in the beginning of your conversation, you learn that your prospect is in a very bad financial situation, you might want to find out whether they could even get funding in order to change their situation. Obviously, if they can't, you are wasting everyone's time, and the reality is that you cannot help them.

You could ask a question like, *"Ms. Kyle, if you were able to find something that could get you what you're looking for, what type of funding would you have to put into it?"*

Notice how you just shifted the focus onto them and away from you? Now they need to sell *you*. Do you see the difference in this approach?

Now let's move on to the part where you'll qualify them *during* the sales conversation.

The following are questions you can ask them then. These are very light, neutral questions designed to tactfully motivate them to move forward with you.

> *"Why is that important to you now though?"*
> *"How would that make you feel to do that?"*
> *"Is this important for to change your situation?"*
> *"How important is it for you to solve this problem?"*
> *"How do you see this being beneficial to you and your company?"*
> *"What are some ways this could help you?"*
> *"If you could . . . what would it do for you personally?"*
> *"How important is this for you?"*
> *"Is this what you're possibly looking for?"*
> *"Are you good with this?"*
> *"Would you agree with this?"*
> *"Does that possibly work for you?"*
> *"Would this be appropriate for your situation?"*
> *"Would this help you?"*
> *"Why though?"*

You never know how a conversation is going to go, and you can't predict the order in which things are revealed, but you can certainly try to steer it with all this knowledge.

Asking questions can save both you and your potential prospects a ton of time—especially if you travel for work.

We see so many salespeople waste precious selling time driving hours to see a prospect that might not even be qualified to buy their solution. Stop doing this now if you want to be at the top in sales.

Before you make a trip that zaps you of significant selling time, you'll want to get at least some smaller commitments from the prospect. Here are some examples of qualifying questions to ask your prospect so you don't waste travel time if you have to travel to appointments by car or by plane.

> **Prospect:** *"Can you come to our offices in Atlanta and do a demo for the owner to see?"*
>
> **New Model Salesperson:** *"Possibly. Now let's suppose I do come out to your office for a day. You're able to pull the owner and the other decision makers together for me to do a demo in person and everyone finds that we can solve this problem you've talked to me about. What do you see happening next?"*

Now at this point, you are going to get one of these answers:

- We would do business with you for sure.
- We would have to run it by our committee/corporate.
- We would have to see if we could get the budget for it.
- We would have to compare it to what we have now with our current vendor.
- I'm not really sure what would happen.

If you get the *first response*, then you should make the trip and do the demo.

If you get any of the other responses, you should not commit your time and resources because there are too many obstacles in the way over which you have no control.

Before you travel to that prospect you need to *find a way to remove those obstacles*. Removing those obstacles will make it much easier for you to get a commitment once you are meeting the prospect face-to-face.

OK, so now you're face-to-face. Let's look at an example dialogue to see the sequencing in full play, starting with a consequence question, then a qualifying question, and then transitioning into presenting while incorporating what the prospects told you they want.

> **New Model Salesperson:** *"Alex, can I ask you another question?"*
>
> **Prospect:** *"Sure, go ahead."*
>
> **New Model Salesperson:** *"And I hate to ask you this because I have enjoyed what you told me, but what are you going to do if nothing changes? I mean, if you keep getting the same results you're getting now from your lead generation for the next two to three years?"*

Or:

"What if you don't do anything about this, though, and you keep getting these low-quality leads to your sales team and that team keeps stagnating for another three, six, or even twelve months?" [Repeat what they said their problem was here.]

Prospect: *"Well, I am not sure. We would really have to cut back on expanding our business for sure."*

New Model Salesperson: *"Are you willing to settle for that?"*

Prospect: *"Oh, no way, we have to do something about this."*

New Model Salesperson: *"How important is it for you to change your situation and start getting higher quality leads so you can make more money to expand your company?"*

Prospect: *"Oh, it's very important."*

New Model Salesperson: *"Why now though?"*

Prospect: *"Well, we have to get serious about this. I'm tired of this other company we have been using . . . they just keep telling us it will get better, but it doesn't."*

New Model Salesperson: *"Is that having an impact on your company?"*

Prospect: *"Yes, for sure. We want to expand, but the lack of sales from not having better leads is hurting us."*

New Model Salesperson: *"Time for a change possibly?"*

Prospect: *"Yes, for sure."*

Here's the *transition* point.

Toward the end of the engagement stage, after you have asked them a very powerful, profound consequence question, go ahead and ask them a qualifying question, especially if they have not been very engaged throughout the sales conversation. On the flip side, if they have repeatedly qualified themselves with the answers they've already given you, you may not even have to ask them qualifying questions. That's why you need to listen carefully.

When you use your engagement stage questions, you will get a zoomed in, precise picture of their situation—wrinkles, flaws, blemishes, and all. How does that help you? You start to see what their answers mean, and you will be able to offer them the right benefits, features, and advantages your solution offers to solve their problems.

Five things happen during the engagement stage:

1. You'll start building trust, which will ultimately strengthen your relationship.
2. You'll learn exactly what your customer is looking for.
3. You'll help your potential customer think about their problems and what they want, to help them persuade themselves to want to make a change by purchasing your product or service.

Before we go on to the other two, about that change, they will want to make that change with—yep, you guessed it—you! Doing this right will eliminate your competition because you are now the "trusted authority" in your industry, and they will never go to anyone else!

4. You'll find out what emotions they're feeling, and these will be the "why" behind what they're looking for. You'll do this by asking emotion-based questions or feeling questions, and then you'll strategically introduce some urgency to help your prospect move forward.

And last, but by no means least:

5. You'll find out *whether* you can help them by qualifying them. You need to be sure that they actually want to change their situation in order to fulfill their need for what they told you they wanted.

With New Model techniques, you'll be able to eliminate objections and rejection completely. However, if you find that you are still getting several objections or rejections, it's likely because you keep going back to the old model of selling. Breaking old habits is hard, but see how fast you'll break them when you start losing sales.

If you keep using traditional sales techniques, the bad habits of presenting your solution or talking about how great your product and company is too early in your conversation, you'll get rejected most of the time. Resist doing this. Put a rubber band on your wrist and snap yourself every time you go back into pitch mode in which you talk about you and your product to present your solution before you find out what their problems are. It works and comes off a lot less psychotic than slapping yourself.

Write the following phrase down and keep it in front of you at your office so you can see it daily. Make a meme out of it with a picture of Snoopy, cross-stitch it into your beer koozie, or make a bumper sticker out of it; whatever motivates you. And never forget it: *Selling is the art of finding and solving problems by asking skilled questions and listening for the answers.*

Your sales conversation should be similar to a chill conversation you would have with a friend—except that it will be a very *skilled* conversation too. Chill and skill and let's move on to the transition and presentation phase, shall we?

Chapter 10

The Transitional Stage

The key to making good movies is to pay attention
to the transition between scenes.
—Steven Soderbergh

N ow that you're armed with a Wikipedia-worthy amount of information on your potential prospect, this is the strategic moment in the
sales process where you are ready for your close-up—ready to present
your solution. But remember, presenting is only 10 percent of the New Model
of Selling. It's where you receive feedback and match your offerings to what
they have told you they are looking for. This is the point where you'll piece
together all of their logical and emotional needs into a jigsaw of justifiable sales.
This will allow you to show your prospects that you have a real understanding
of what they want.

Right after your consequence questions, you will immediately transition into
your presentation if you are in a one-call close. Now if you are in a two-call close,
a multiple-call close, or operating in a more complex B2B selling environment,
then you will still transition, but you'll transition into the next step. That might
be giving a demo, outlining a proposal, or setting up another meeting; it just
depends on what industry you're in and what you sell.

You will transition with this statement and ask questions like this:

> **New Model Salesperson:** *"**Based on what you told me**, Alex, what we are doing here at XYZ Lead Company would work for you. **You know how you were saying** you want a higher qualified lead and right now your sales are down by 37 percent because the leads you're getting don't have much money, and because of that, it's causing you to feel . . . **I think you mentioned a little bit of stress sometimes?"**

Now, why would you downplay the stress he talked about by saying "a little bit of stress"?

Because your prospect will fight back by saying, *"Oh no, you have no idea how much stress it's causing."* This causes them to feel their pain even more. Not that you want to inflict pain on them, but you want them to reveal to you what a pain it truly is so you can jump in and help relieve that pain. See where we're going with this?

If, on the flip side, you said, *"This is causing you a lot of stress,"* certain personalities will then go on the defense and say, *"Well, it's not that bad"* and say the complete opposite. Especially if they are an A-type personality who doesn't want to look weak.

So you always want to downplay, with language like "a little bit of stress," "a little bit frustrated sometimes," "a little bit worried sometimes," or "a little bit of anxiety." Do you see how that works? A little bit, right?

> **Prospect:** *"A little bit of stress? You have no idea the stress; it's so stressful, I can't even sleep at night right now."*
>
> **New Model Salesperson:** *"What's that doing to you?"*
>
> **Prospect:** *"I feel like I'm going to have a heart attack, actually, my wife is very concerned."*
>
> **New Model Salesperson:** *"I see, so it's important for you to do something then?"*
>
> **Prospect:** *"You got that right, buddy."*
>
> **New Model Salesperson:** *"Well, with your permission, what we do at XYZ Company is we . . ."*

So let's look at how you'll transition. Remember to say:

> *"Based on what you told me, what we are doing might actually work for you . . ."*
> *"Because you know how you said . . ."*
> *". . . and because of that it's making you feel . . ."*
> *"This is what we do . . ."*

Here's a more specific one:

> *"Amy,* **based on what you told me**, *what we are doing might actually work for you* **because you know how you said** *you want to find a home in a better neighborhood, and right now you like your house, but because of some recent break-ins in the area* **it's caused you to feel**—*I think you had said* **a little bit** *of worry sometimes . . ."*

Keep the conversation oriented around them and solving their problems.

Constructing Your Proposal and Presentation

Now that you've got your prospect's attention focused on them solving their problems, you'll need to be sure your proposal and presentation do the same with a three-step structure that works no matter what you sell.

You don't need to be David Blaine or Copperfield to effectively pull off a proposal. It's not magic; it's certainly not an illusion; it's completely real. Now, if you sell cars, insurance, or D2D alarms, you won't be making proposals for your prospects; this is mostly for more complex B2B selling. Once we get through the proposal part, we will go through the three-step formula for putting together a killer presentation no matter what you sell.

Rule Number 1: Never give a prospect a proposal without understanding what their problems are, and without knowing whether or not they have the budget/funding/money to solve the problem.

You should live by this; there are no exceptions to this rule, even if you have a prospect who says, *"Can you just send me over a proposal with your pricing in it?"* You must never fall prey to this with a prospect. If a potential customer asks for a proposal up front and early in the call before you have discovered what their situation is, you simply reply:

> *"I'd be open to putting together a proposal for you. Now, to be frank, I'm not quite sure we could even help you yet. Could I ask a few questions about your situation to be able to put something together for you that might be useful? Would that be appropriate?"*

Then you start asking your situation questions to find out more about their present situation. It's as easy as that!

Rule Number 2: Your proposals should lay out the key two to three problems they told you about during the engagement stage of the sales conversation. This reminds them of the issues they want to solve and brings back the pain they feel from those problems. You want them to re-live that pain! Ouch, we know. But, again, it's their pain, not any pain you're inflicting on them.

The proposal should also have the key two to three objectives they want to accomplish as a company, or if you're selling more B2C, make sure to include what it is they want to accomplish personally for some industries.

This creates a proposal that shows that the salesperson was present in the conversation, showing the prospect that you have a complete understanding of their situation and how to solve it for them. Clever, isn't it?

The proposal restates the value to the prospect of achieving their objectives by solving their problems.

By restating the value, it helps you provide context for the sale so that the price for your solution seems like small change compared to them being able to achieve their objectives by solving the issue(s) that is (are) holding them back.

You always want the value of solving the prospects' problems and achieving their objectives to be at least ten times the cost of your offer. No pun intended; it's absolutely priceless.

For a company solving a problem that is costing them $15 million a year in lost revenue, a $250,000 solution will seem quite small to them if you are positioning it correctly. Going over this value with the prospect during your presentation and the proposal makes it a logical next step for them to do business with you. And always have more than one option for them to accomplish their objectives.

Every proposal you send out should provide at least three options for them to accomplish their goals. Most proposals we have seen typically only offer one option. This loses many prospects, as even with the best questions, you still will not be able to read the prospect's mind 100 percent. That is why it's important for you to provide three options for them to work with your company. Rewind to your school days when multiple-choice tests were always better than fill-in-the-blanks because you had a greater chance of getting it right. Same goes for your proposals.

Option 1: A basic, lower-priced option that is still profitable to your company.

Option 2: A middle-of-the-road option that is your core offering where most prospects fall into.

Option 3: A high-priced option that is the premium choice.

Setting up the proposal with these options helps your prospect to make a well-informed decision. The power of the premium option is not just that it's highly profitable to your organization or that some prospects will choose it, but it also makes the middle-of-the-road option with your core offering seem like a great bargain to the prospect. This will help you make not only more sales but much larger sales. Because, really, who doesn't like a good bargain?

Make the Proposal a Basic Contract/Agreement

You can kill two birds with one stone and also make your proposals serve as a signable agreement to get the ball rolling while you are waiting on the agreement to be drawn up, which sometimes can take a week or longer.

Remember, the more steps you add to the sales process, the more chance of it falling apart.

If someone in the organization has to approve the proposal, and then it takes a week or two to draw up the contract, there is more of a chance that the prospect might change their mind and go in a different direction.

You should always make the buying process easy for your potential customers. Give your prospect the opportunity to sign the proposal as the first step in doing business with you. Make sure your proposals serve as a contract. They don't have to be legally binding, but it's a smaller commitment to get them started in the process.

Crafting a Winning Presentation

As Lilly Walters, author of *Secrets of Successful Speakers* said, "The success of your presentation will be judged not by the knowledge you send but by what the listener receives." Follow the three-step structure on how to whip up a winning presentation that connects the dots for every prospect you talk to and you're on your way to ensuring that your listener receives the message that you are the way to go.

But first, the most important, crucial rule: *never, ever* email the proposal over to the prospect before going through the presentation because if they don't like something in it, you are DOA. Why? Because you're not there to clarify or help them overcome any concerns! You *always* want to go over the proposal and presentation face-to-face, on Zoom, or over the phone.

The best two options there are to go over the proposal face-to-face or over Zoom so you can see their body language and be physically (or virtually) present while going over the options and addressing any concerns they might have. If you can do that, you have a *much* better opportunity to close that sale.

Here are some general rules to follow:

1. Give the presentation around the problems/challenges/issues that the prospect mentioned in the engagement process. So many salespeople try to cram the entire solution into a presentation. That is how fifty-page proposals and ninety-minute presentations happen. Doing that will turn most of your prospects off quickly. It goes in one ear and out the other as they lose focus and start texting their colleagues asking what's for lunch or what time is happy hour.

   Instead, your potential customers want to know *whether* you can solve their problems. They just care about you solving their key challenges that are holding them back from achieving results. So stop presenting all the features and benefits that have nothing to do with solving the prospects' problem(s). Only present directly on the issues the prospect mentioned during the engagement stage of the sales conversation.

   You have to tailor each presentation to each prospect's challenges. Never do cookie-cutter presentations; it will make your prospect feel like you do not understand their needs because, frankly, if you're copying and pasting presentations, you clearly don't.

2. Use case studies to reinforce how your solution solves your prospects' problems. This is primarily for B2B presentations. If you sell cars, boats, final expense insurance, or you are in several other industries, you probably wouldn't really use case studies. Case studies are primarily used more for a B2B sale, but sometimes can be used in B2C sales.

    Using case studies is powerful if done correctly. You can show real-life examples of other clients who were in similar situations and how your solution was able to solve their problems. People love before and after pictures, literally and figuratively.

    The case study should show the problems the prospect faced, what your solution did to solve those problems, and what the results of the work ended up being for that prospect.

    Include real numbers that can be objectively quantified. Remember your prospect cares most about results, not features and benefits. They want to know what your solution will do for them and how it will help them get to where they want to go. Superfluous drivel will only give them more time to think about the other salespeople they can call to help them solve their problems while you're busy rambling.

3. Ask "checking for agreement questions" throughout the presentation. Most sales presentations are an hour or more monologue with the salesperson talking most of the time about all the great features and benefits of their solution, and how they have the best company, the best customer service, the best quality, the best delivery, and the best this and the best that. You still there? Exactly. If your eyes didn't roll you into a deep sleep by now, it's only a matter of time. This sales drivel is the Pinto of sales. It's a lemon, and you can't add vodka to it to make a spiked lemonade. It's also basically what every salesperson says about their product or service.

    How many salespeople do you know whose sales pitch includes that pesky fact that their product/service is only fourth or fifth best in the market? We hear crickets on that one because the answer is no one, right? They all say they are the best, so prospects have built up defensive mechanisms when they hear this type of stale sales spiel. Doing this is a disaster if you want to be a top performer in sales.

To prevent this epic sales fail from happening, you want to ask checking for agreement questions. These questions engage the customer during the presentation and create feedback and buy-in. They increase the effectiveness of your presentations tenfold. They make you appear credible in their eyes and more of an authority.

Here are some examples:

> *"Does that make sense?"*
> *"Are we on the same page?"*
> *"What are your thoughts on that?"*
> *"Are you with me on this?"*
> *"Do you see how that works?"*
> *"Do you see how that could help you?"*
> *"How do you see that helping you the most?"*
> *"Any questions on that?"*
> *"Is there anything else I should add?"*

These questions help you keep a pulse on how the presentation is going with the prospect. It serves as a dialogue that keeps the prospect engaged in the conversation.

It makes the prospect feel they are part of the process and much more likely to buy. *Do you see how that works?* (Heh, we just asked you a checking for agreement question and hopefully you either nodded your head or shouted out an emphatic "heck, yeah!")

During the presentation, you should be asking at least five to ten of these types of questions to make sure the potential customer is on the same page.

Most salespeople present 50 percent of the sales process. This is way, way too much. The presentation stage should only be about 10 percent of the sale. It should be about presenting back the challenges and problems they told you about during the engagement stage and presenting back how your solution can solve those challenges. Nothing more, nothing less.

The amount of information the prospect needs to know will always be much less than what a salesperson thinks it is.

Now it's time to reveal our winning three-step formula to crafting those winning presentations that connect *all* the dots in your prospects' minds.

We typically want to have three to four pillars of problems, how we solve those for people like them, and what that means to them.

1. So either repeat back their problem which you will want to do probably in the first and second pillars, or put problems in their minds that they may not have even know they had in the first place.

    "Remember how you said that you were having this [repeat back the problem they revealed to you here]*?"*
    "One of the biggest problems that people have when they are trying to . . ."

    or

    "One of the biggest problems that people have when they come to us is they [plug in the problem here] *"*

    or

    "One of the biggest problems that people have when they come to us is that they don't know how to/they're not able to/they don't have sufficient [insert whatever you are selling here and repeat back their problem and the consequence of how the problem affects them] *"*

2. Go over how your product, service, or program solves a particular part of their problem.

    "So the way we solve that for our clients like you is we [insert how you can fix their issues here] *"*

3. Repeat back the advantages and benefits of what it will do for them or
    what it will mean for them once their problems are solved.

"And what that means to you is [repeat the advantages and benefits here] *"*

Let's say you sell real estate training that teaches people how to invest in
real estate.

For each industry, there will be tweaks and differences in how you would say
this, but here's a sample script of a presentation:

> *"**Remember when you mentioned** that right now you want to get your first
> investment property, but you're limited with your capital, so you would
> have to go really slow? One of the biggest problems most people have when
> they're looking to invest in real estate is that they don't understand their
> different financing options and how to get into a property with little to no
> money down."*

[Repeat what the problem does to them here] and continue:

> *"So they get stuck at saving and only being able to pick up one property every
> one to two years, so it takes them decades to become a full-time investor.*
> > *"**The way we solve that for our clients** is we teach them eight
> different strategies on how to profit on any deal that's in front of them
> that includes: How to Wholesale, Do Traditional Rentals, Lease Options,
> Wraps, Sub Tails, Group Homes, Airbnbs, and Short-Term Rentals.*
> > *"**What this means to you is** you're not letting any deal fall through
> the cracks, and you're not having to use your own money, apply for hard
> money loans, or deal with personal bank loans. So that way you can scale
> your portfolio/business quickly and not be restricted by money.*
> > *"Are you with me on that?"*

Let's look at another example in a completely different industry. This is from
the marriage or relationship industry selling marriage counseling and relationship

building, yikes. But it's completely doable. Jeremy worked with a client in this field who went from closing 30 percent to 61 percent in sixty days! She doubled her sales in *two* months. Boom!

Here's that sample script:

> "**Remember when you said** *you want to feel connected and supported in your marriage? And right now, it feels like you are caught in a hamster wheel where you and your husband (blow up, shut down, argue) all the time, which is causing you to feel disconnected and question whether you should even still be married?*
>
> "**One of the biggest problem clients** *have when they come to us is that they don't know* how *to change the reactive relational pattern they are experiencing in their marriage.*
>
> "**So, the way we solve this** *in Dr. Sun's Heal Your Relationships from the Inside Out program is starting with the Conflict Triggers Assessment.*
>
> "*Every couple has a unique dance. In this first pillar of the program, we will help you map out every single part of your dance so you can see it before it even happens, and then we teach you custom one degree shifts that will change the trajectory of your dance.*
>
> "**And what this means for you is**, *once you can see the whole dance and name it, understand both of your conflict personas and how they work together, and you know which 1 percent shift to use in which moment to heal your triggers, your whole conflict dance changes. At that point, your playful connection starts to come back like you had when you were first dating, so your marriage starts to heal itself for you and your family.*
>
> "*Does that make sense?*"

This presentation is so good, it not only makes sense, but it made her double her sales in two months. That's what we're talking about here!

These winning presentations are key, but they're not always an immediate shoe-in. Any successful salesperson is aware that they will come head-to-head with objections and pushbacks. Don't fret. You'll get through them with your New Model mastery.

Understanding the Dreaded "Objection"

So you crushed your presentation, but yet, your prospect still has (legitimate) concerns, which can come across as objections, but let's call them the kinder, gentler *concerns* so you can continue to forge ahead positively. Remind yourself that it's not personal; it's not a rejection of you. When you hear these concerns, reel in your desire to react. Most salespeople fly off the cuff at this point instead of working to uncover what the objection—er, concern—actually means.

Realize that now is not the time to go back into selling mode to try to persuade them with logical facts on why your solution is good for them. Been there, done that, and almost got the T-shirt too. Hang on a minute. You're almost there.

It's time to use the same principles and methods you have learned from the New Model NEPQ system. If you have done your work correctly and gone deep into the conversation with your prospect, then most, if not all, objections slash concerns will have been eliminated during the engagement stage of the process.

If you do get an objection at this stage, don't let it slow your roll; just look at it as a concern. Try to understand the customer and put yourself in their shoes as they determine whether what you're offering is only an empty *promise* of a better future. Understand that they have to make that commitment before you deliver what you promised. Quite possibly, their objection is nothing more than a request for more information.

There's also the possibility that their objection may just be a request for a few simple tweaks to what you originally offered them. Perhaps they want a few changes made to the terms of what you are offering. Don't count it out just yet! Objections, or concerns, are sometimes requests for any of the following:

1. The price of the solution you're offering.
2. The timing of your solution.
3. The follow-up, or how they will be serviced.
4. The quality of what you're offering; perhaps they want you to commit more time or more resources like personnel to meet their needs.

In B2B sales, habit or, "we have always done it that way" is a big objection. So is satisfaction. They may think they are happy with what they are using and don't feel they are in the market for something new.

The latter isn't as hard to crack as the mystery of the origins of Stonehenge. It all boils down to questioning. Good questions to ask to help them overcome this way of thinking are aplenty and include: *"You've already reached big numbers and milestones. Tell me, where do you want to go from here in terms of future improvements in . . . ?"* or *"Can I ask, how does your ideal situation compare to what you have now with this vendor you are using?"*

But wait! There's more:

> *"Back when you chose to work with that company* [current vendor] *what was your selection criteria if I could ask? In what ways has that changed as you look at your needs today though? Can I ask what you'd change if you could?"* or *"Can I ask in what ways could the company you use do better for you than what they are doing now?"*

Let's say that your prospect decides to stay with their current vendor and told you they will stay with the company they are already using at the end of your entire sales process. Rather than just giving up, a good way to restart that conversation would be by asking this question: *"How would I be able to communicate to you that you might be making the wrong decision without you getting upset with me?"*

There is no point in proceeding to help them overcome their objections if you don't completely understand their objection. Most salespeople will think that they've heard every single objection that ever existed in their universe and assume that they know exactly what each objection means. (Spoiler alert: they don't.) Then they proceed to deliver a canned response.

If the customer says, *"It's too expensive,"* the average salesperson believes they know what that means. But the question has to be asked: do they really know what that specific objection means in the customer's mind? Is this example a clear objection?

What does this *"It's too expensive"* objection actually mean?

Does it mean it's too expensive to pay *right now?*

Does it mean it's too expensive compared to a competitor?

Does it mean it's too expensive to pay up front and they need a payment plan?

Does it mean they don't have the budget for it at all?

It's too expensive in relation to what?

When you don't know exactly what your prospect is talking about, your assumptions will end up costing you a sale unlike that time you tried to order a "cone" from the drive-thru and instead got a Coke. But that's just silly semantics. In sales, *always* be sure to fully understand the objection.

Here's an example of how most salespeople who use traditional selling skills would react to an objection:

> **Prospect:** *"These TVs are just too expensive for our company to buy in bulk."*
>
> **Average Salesperson:** *"Too expensive? They are really not expensive if you think about the added benefits they will bring to your customers in your restaurant. Your customers will like the picture quality compared to what you are using now. They will want to come to your restaurant to watch sports just because of the picture quality of your TVs."*
>
> **Prospect:** *"Well, I still believe they are just too much to pay for."*
>
> **Average Salesperson:** *"Keep in mind that you get twenty-four-hour customer service with our TVs, so, if anything happens, we are available twenty-four hours a day for you."*

This conversation will go to a blank screen, absolutely nowhere, and alas, the sale is lost because of the way the salesperson communicated.

Regardless of the features and benefits the salesperson talked about, the objection is still weighing on the mind of the prospect. The customer is thinking, *"I've told this guy twice now that I think it's too expensive, and he's just not listening to me."*

In the New Model process, you have to respect and value what your prospects say. This undoubtedly means that you must understand what your potential customer actually means when they give you an objection. Unless you're a psychic, there's no way you know what the customer means when the customer hasn't clarified the meaning to you. But if you think you do, we can see your sales future right here, right now, and it looks bleak.

For the dialogue to work properly, you have to lose your assumption that you understand the objection. When your prospect gives you an objection, they are basically telling you that it's a risk for them. This should be a red flag in your mind, and at this point, your job is to help your prospect overcome their own objection to move them forward to purchase your product or service.

Remember to go beyond this objection by going deeper:

> **Prospect:** *"This is just too expensive for our company."*
> **New Model Salesperson:** *"What do you mean by 'it's too expensive'?"*
> **Prospect:** *"Well, another company I am looking at is 12 percent cheaper for the same product."*

Do you see how that works? The salesperson now knows what the prospect means when they say it's too expensive.

In other situations, it could mean something completely different. It could mean: *"We just don't have the budget for this right now,"* *"Your quote would be too high for us once we add in repairs and maintenance costs,"* or *"Once we hire someone to run your equipment, it takes us over what we have allocated for this."*

Can you see how each of these answers reveals a different reason for the objection of *"This is too expensive"*?

But you're not done yet. You also have to make sure that you uncover the reason that's actually behind the concern. What caused them to have the concern? If you understand their objections, you are far better prepared to ask the right questions to help them overcome their own concerns.

> **Prospect:** *"This proposal is just too expensive for the company."*
> **New Model Salesperson:** *"How do you mean it's too expensive?"* or *"In what way?"*
> **Prospect:** *"Well, the most we could pay for this service is about $10K a month maximum, and you're quoting me around $15K a month."*
> **New Model Salesperson:** *"Can I ask you how you arrived at that monthly figure of $10K a month?"*
> **Prospect:** *"That is what our CEO has allocated us to be able to spend on this type of service because of cutbacks in our department from the merger."*

A ha! *Now* the salesperson can see the picture more clearly than before. The meaning of *"It's too expensive"* is that the CEO has only allocated $10K monthly due to cutbacks because the company has recently gone through a merger.

With this extra knowledge, the salesperson may be able to negotiate a different agreement on price, perhaps by changing service options from the original offer or by giving them a different type of service that matches their budget. Also something to realize here is that there is always money! The money already exists. Lights are on, floors are being mopped, and employees are being paid. Money is just allocated to priorities. So your question is really not one of finding more money for them to buy your solution, but it's a matter of how good you are about getting them to view your solution as a priority and to move that money that already exists somewhere else to you!

So NEPQ questions can allow your prospect to view your solution as the priority and move it from one department to another so they can pay for *your* solution to solve *their* problems and get them to where they want to be!

Here are a few great questions for this scenario:

> *"Do you feel like the budget you've been given is sufficient to solve this problem?"*

Or

> *"With cost being the most important thing to your CEO, can I ask how that compares to your company actually getting results and being able to solve this problem though?"*

These questions provoke them to think that maybe they need to get funds elsewhere, or to tap into a different department to be able to invest with you to solve their problems. They will likely be inspired to go get the funds to do it even if they don't have them just yet. Kids do this with their parents.

> **Kid:** *"Mom, can I get more Robux to play Roblox? I don't have any more of my allowance money."*
>
> **Mom:** *"No."*
>
> **Kid:** *"Dad, can I get more Robux to play Roblox? I don't have any more of my allowance money."*

Dad: *"Ask your mom."*

OK, so in business it's different, but you get the picture. Asking skilled questions about their concern helps you get better information that clarifies their concerns and aides you in finding a solution. You are also helping your potential customer think and overcome their own concerns. You're requesting clarification about their concern so that you can fully understand it.

Here are some clarifying questions you can ask your prospects to better understand exactly what they mean.

> *"How did you arrive at that?"*
> *"Can you tell me more about that?"*
> *"Why do you feel that way?"*
> *"Why do you say that?"*
> *"Can you tell me what you mean exactly by that?"*
> *"When you say . . . , what do you mean by that exactly?"* [Be sure to feed back to them exactly what they said here.]
> *"I'm curious, why did you ask me that?"*
> *"How do you mean exactly?"*
> *"What do you mean by* [repeat back what they said]*?"*
> *"You seem a bit hesitant, what's behind that?"*
> *"Can I ask you where you got your information from?"*

Never, ever assume that you understand what they mean. Do not tell them that you know how they feel. Forget about the "feel, felt, found" technique that too many salespeople use. It's just so overused by salespeople. It's basically answering the objection with a cringey *"Yes, but"* answer.

Truth be told, you have absolutely no clue how they feel. Besides, so many salespeople have been taught to handle objections this way and many of your prospects have heard this same exact sales line before. If you use this outdated technique, most of the time you'll lose your prospect's trust.

When you ask NEPQ, low-key questions, your prospect will answer you and their answers will provide you with the guidance you need to follow up with the appropriate questions that will get them to overcome their own concerns. Because you have acknowledged their concern and have not tried to refute and invalidate it, your customer will notice that you are *very* different from any other salesperson they have dealt with because you have shown an interest in their issue. You, sales slayer, are a rare breed. Success will follow.

Most salespeople just argue and try to position themselves almost in a bullying fashion as they try to sweep the objection under the rug, hoping and praying that the prospect will somehow forget about it. Newsflash: they won't; they'll just forget about you and what you're selling.

At this point, when the potential customer looks at you, they'll see you as the trusted authority, the expert who will listen to them and who cares more about their concern, and then, guess what, their concern starts to minimize. Their objection will still be there, but because of your advanced listening skills, and your ability to stay focused on their world and serving them, instead of being focused on just closing the sale, they'll treat you differently.

Why? Because dealing with you will be far less risky. You are committed to understanding them and what they are looking for. Reacting will not get you far. Ninety-nine percent of salespeople simply react to a prospect's objection. However, a reaction does not give you a plan to proceed that helps your customer overcome their own concerns. In fact, it usually gets you shown the door.

The Suppose Question

So you've skillfully sleuthed your way through your prospect's first concern and the reason behind that concern. But hang on, Sherlock and Nancy Drew, you guys aren't done yet. You now need to learn whether there are any other concerns that could possibly hold them back from doing business with you. And to determine this, you'll need to ask yet another question.

The New Model Salesperson calls this the suppose question. It's designed to uncover whether there are any other concerns. For instance:

> *"Let's suppose we were able to resolve that issue with you. I know it's not resolved right now, but let's just pretend we could. Are there any other issues you might have that you would want to see resolved?"*

Do you see the simplicity in this question? They will either tell you the original concern they told you is the only concern they have, or they will tell you about other concerns they may have.

Check this out:

"Let's suppose we were able to resolve that issue with you."

This question is designed to get your customer to envision both of you working together to resolve their concerns. It's a team effort; hence the wording "with you" and not "for you." Here, both you and your customer are coming up with solutions to resolve their concern together. Cue the Kumbaya right about now. But wait, there's more! There's a sequel to this formula that's so much better than *Jaws: The Revenge.*

Here it is:

"I know it's not resolved right now, but let's just pretend we could."

This part of the question acknowledges that you *respect* their concern. You are also letting them know that their first concern will be addressed and that you're not trying to blow it off. This shows your prospect that you are fully present in the conversation.

"Are there any other issues you might have that you would want to see resolved?"

This question helps you and your prospect separate the first concern from any other concerns they might have.

Here's your script. Be sure to memorize your lines. The more you rehearse, the more natural you'll sound. You won't win any Oscars, but what you'll gain from it will be just as priceless as that golden statue of a naked old dude.

"Let's suppose *we were able to resolve that issue* with *you. I know it's not resolved right now, but let's just pretend we could. Are there any other issues you might have that you would want to see resolved?"*

When you ask the "suppose" question in a calm and relaxed conversational manner, you help your prospect think through their concerns. Your potential customer is now involved in the process. They are helping you understand, and more importantly, they are arriving at a better understanding of themselves at the same time. They have now come to realize that you have listened to them and that you are respecting and understanding their concerns. You're now a team! This is when you'll be prepared to work with them on *overcoming* their concerns.

Handling Demands You Can't Meet

Look, you're good, but you're not *that* good—yet. There will absolutely be times when your prospects will have demands that are beyond your authority or control. What you can do is skillfully handle these demands professionally. Follow these steps and you'll get through it:

> Step 1. Make sure to repeat what your prospect wants.
> > *"John, let me make sure I understand what you want."*
> Step 2. Make sure to include their objection or interest.
> > *"Give me a second while I put this into your perspective . . ."*
> Step 3. Turn down their request by giving them an explanation.
> > *"I want you to know why that's further than I could actually go."*

The *"I want you to know"* statement is a very neutral way of saying no. This language respects your prospect and gets them to think. With the right dialogue, you and your prospect are both open to each other because of the trust you have built with them through the use of your skilled questions and listening ability. Your potential customer needs to know you're thinking about their objection and not just figuring out how to squirm out of it.

Your neutral explanation, along with a few strategic questions, can lead to them understanding and agreeing with you most of the time. They view you as the trusted authority to help them do that, so why would they ever want to go with someone else?

At this point, you want to ask them questions such as the following:

"Would you like to go over with me what I think might work for you?"
"I might have a possible solution to this. Would you like to go over that with me?"

This allows you to invite your potential customers to work out their concerns with you so that, together, both of you can find a solution.

Remember that your potential customer *wants* a solution. With this question, you are both agreeing to come up with a way to get there.

From here, you're going to briefly discuss their concerns using questions from the engagement stage to uncover and explore solutions to their concerns. Your solution awareness questions are very powerful. So you can proceed by asking them the following question:

"How do you see yourself being able to resolve your concern?"

And that right there leads you straight into the part where you're about to bust open the barrier between you and that sale as you Sherpa your prospects to the sales summit that is them figuring out how to overcome their own concerns. There is no altitude sickness at that summit, only the sweet smell of a sale. Keep going. You're almost there.

Help Them Help Themselves

Welcome to the point in the sales conversation where your prospects will start to tell you how they think that they themselves can resolve their concern. Yikes, we know. But you got this. They are telling you this because they are emotionally involved with their problems at this point *because of* the questions you asked them, and they are emotionally invested in wanting to solve their own problems. So, after you discuss what their concern is, you can fire off these questions to get them to resolve their concern themselves:

"Let's suppose that it wasn't what you thought it was?"
"Suppose you could . . . ?"
"What if we could . . . ?"
"What if you could . . . ?"

Then you'll just have to plug in an alternative view to theirs. Let's say you sell health coaching services and that your potential customer's concern is that he has already tried weight loss programs in the past, but he hasn't had any success because he felt he didn't have the support he needed.

> **New Model Salesperson:** *"Mr. Jones, if there was a way you could get that support you said you needed and have a coach who would assist you weekly to make sure you actually lost the weight so that you can live longer for your grandkids* [here's where you plug in what they said they wanted]*, would you feel comfortable working with us on helping you get to that point?"*

Here are some other questions that you can ask to make sure your prospective customers are on the same page and that they have overcome their own concerns. Realize that at this point, you are just checking for agreement before you ask a few of your committing or closing questions to bring them to purchase your solution, i.e., your product/service.

> *"Would you be comfortable with that?"*
> *"How does that look so far to you?"*
> *"Would that work for you?"*
> *"Would that be appropriate?"*
> *"Would that help you?"*
> *"Is there anything else you would like to address with me at this point?"*

This last question, *"Is there anything else you would like to address at this point?"* is important to ask after you have helped them resolve their first concern but remember: don't assume their first concern was their only concern.

How to Address the "I Can't Afford It" Concern

What about if they reply with a track from the potential prospects' greatest hits: *"We can't afford it," "We don't have a budget for that,"* or *"Your price is too high"*?

Here you go:

Prospect: *"We like your product, but at this time, we just can't afford it."*

New Model Salesperson: *"Tell me, if you did have the money, would this be something that would work for you?"*

Prospect: *"Yeah, for sure."*

New Model Salesperson: *"Why do you feel it would though?"*

Prospect: *"Well, we like* [your service or product]*, but we just don't have the money for it."*

New Model Salesperson: *"I can appreciate that money might be an issue for you. How do you think you can resolve that where you can find the money so that you can . . . ?"*

Here you just plug in what they said they wanted. You are tying them getting the funding/money to having what they said they wanted. If they don't get the funding/money, then they can't have what they said they wanted.

Because they have trust in you at this point, many times when you ask them this question, they will be the ones to come up with ways on how they can get the funds together. When you do this correctly, they'll think about using a credit card, getting a loan, refinancing their house, borrowing from their 401(k), investments, or getting their boss to take money from a different department to invest in your solution.

However, if they cannot come up with ways on how they can get the money, you can ask them, *"What other avenues do you have to find the funding so that you can . . . "* Once again, you are just filling in what they said they wanted.

Here are some examples:

If you sell home security systems: *"What other avenues do you have to find the funding to protect your home and family from intruders breaking in?"*

If you sell health coaching or supplements: *"What other avenues do you have to find the funding to be able to lose these eighty pounds so, like you mentioned, you can watch your kids grow up?"*

If you sell rental or commercial properties: *"What other avenues do you have to find the funding to purchase this rental property so you can get a greater return on your money?"*

If you sell real estate: *"What other avenues do you have to find the funding to use as a down payment so you can get your family into this safer neighborhood?"*

If you sell lead services or marketing: *"What other avenues do you have to find the funding to start getting a higher quality of lead so your salespeople can make more sales for you?"*

If you sell life insurance: *"What other avenues do you have to find the funding to increase the financial protection for your wife and kids when something happens to you?"*

Here's a quick question for you: What do you think is best to do if your prospect still can't come up with ways to find the funding themselves? No, it's not time to abandon ship. You don't quit. The sale is more alive right now than Tupac and fat Elvis. What you do is you make suggestions.

Share with them how your other clients have been able to find the funds and then you can ask them whether that would help them or work for them.

"A lot of our clients just use their credit card or get some type of loan to get the funding. Would that help you?"

"A lot of our clients just use funds from their 401(k) or other investments to get the funding. Would that work for you?"

Here's an industry-specific example so you can see how the structure works for what you sell. Just plug in your product or service here.

In this example, the salesperson is selling e-commerce training.

"Tell me, if you did have the funds, is this something that would work for you?" (Spoiler Alert: they will always say yes.)

"Why though?" (Channel your best Oscar-winning actor voice here.)

*"OK, so I can appreciate that money might be an issue for you. How do you think you can resolve that where you can find funding **so you can start making profits in your e-commerce store?**"* (Let them come up with ways.)

If they cannot figure it out:

"What other avenues do you have to find funding to start a business so you can make more money?"

If they still can't come up with ways:

"Have you ever considered putting it on a credit card and just paying it off when we start making profits after we set everything up with you?"

Here is the complete generic version. Once again, plug in what you sell to this structure:

"Tell me, if you did have the funding/budget/money, is this something that would work for you?
"Why do you feel it would though?"
"I can appreciate that money might be an issue from what you told me. Tell me, how do you think you can resolve that so you can [repeat back what they want here]*?"*
"What other avenues do you have to find the budget/funding/money so you can [repeat back what they said they wanted here]*?"*
"Can I make a suggestion?"

And you will simply suggest what other clients of yours do to find the funds to solve the problem.

Voilà! It's not over yet. But wait, there's more!

How to Address the "I Need to Think It Over" Concern

How do you overcome the "I need to think it over concern"? Like Billy Joel taking requests for "Piano Man," this is one you probably get quite a bit. How do you disarm the prospect where they won't push back, where they will open up to you and tell you what their real concerns are? What do most reps say when they get this concern at the end? Most reps say something like this, or variations similar to this:

Prospect: *"We really like this, but we need to think it over."*

Average Salesperson: *"I'm confused. You said* [and they repeat back what they said they wanted]. *What do you want to think about, or what do you need to think over?"*

You know what that is? It's a logic-based trap to get the prospect to admit that they said they wanted to change their situation, but hang on a minute! Do people buy on logic or emotion? You'll take emotion for the win, of course, and while you may win over a few with logic, you are losing a *ton* of sales that you could be making if you knew how to use human behavior to your advantage, and really to their advantage as well.

Realize that when your prospect says, *"I want to think it over,"* most of the time this is because you have not asked the right questions at the right time in that sales conversation to help them see clearly what their problems are, the root cause of the problems, and how it will affect them if they don't do anything.

Remember you can't *tell* them that, you have to ask the right questions that allow them to tell *themselves* that, and when they tell themselves why they need to change their situation, they persuade themselves, and it creates massive urgency for them to want to purchase *now*, not weeks or months down the road.

On the flip side, when they feel that their problem isn't insurmountable because your questioning was off and you couldn't help them see that it actually is, it causes them to feel that the problem they have might not be that bad after all, or maybe they feel you cannot get them the results they want. There has to be a gap in their mind between where they are now (their current situation, their current state) compared to where they want to be, and we call that the objective state.

What's holding them back from getting what they want? All these problems that your questions have helped them discover! The larger the gap, the more urgency there is for them to buy now, not later. And that gap can only be created in their minds by the questions you've asked them!

Here is an example of how to resolve this concern:

Prospect: *"This sounds good, but let me think it over."*
New Model Salesperson: *"That's not a problem. What's your timeframe on getting back to me in the next day or two just to see if I would be available for you?"*

Now, why on earth would you not try to overcome that objection right here? Why would you try to set up a second call? *Because it takes the sales pressure right out of the conversation.* It disarms the prospect and causes them to let their guard down. It also positions you as busy with other clients, as if you don't need the sale. You're detached. Yes! When it comes to this relationship courting, detachment is a very good thing!

Prospect: *"I guess I could call you in a few days."*

Uhh, not so much. You need a scheduled time, no waffling.

New Model Salesperson: *"Well possibly.* But *what I can do, if you have your calendar handy, is I can pull up mine and have you book a specific time with me, that way you don't have to chase me down and vice versa, would that be appropriate?"*

This is called a calendar commitment. It works every time and shows that you are not desperate, you are busy, and that you have tons of clients whose problems you are helping solve like the Dr. Phil of sales.

Now after you book the appointment, you ask this:

New Model Salesperson: *"Now, before I go, what were you wanting to go over in your mind* [this is a better, nicer way of saying, "What do you want to think about?"], *just so I know what questions you might have when we talk tomorrow?"*

Now brace yourself because this is the key at this point; this is the part where they are going to tell you what their real concern is. They might say, *"Well I'm just concerned about,"* or *"I'm just not understanding this part,"* or *"I'm not sure if I can get the money for this."*

Then you will be able to clarify their concern, ask a diffusing question, and then discuss it like two people who are trying to work out a solution together, and most of the time close the sale on that call. Boom!

How to Address the "Can you Send Me References?" Question

Another of the greatest hits of objections, and if they ask you this, 99 percent of the time, it's because they have a concern, that they don't trust that you can get them the results they said they wanted. Why? Because you don't know the right questions to ask that create that certainty in their mind where they view you as the expert, as the trusted authority, and that's exactly why they ask you for references!

Not all requests for references are because of mistrust, though. References from satisfied customers can be a great tool to help a prospect move forward with your solution. However, it can also be just a way for the prospect to get rid of you, the pesky salesperson.

You have to ask *qualifying questions* to really find out whether this potential customer is serious about changing their situation, whether they have a legitimate concern, or whether they are just wasting your time.

Here are some examples of questions to ask if they ask the "Send me some references" question:

> **Prospect:** *"Can you send me some references from other clients you have?"*
> **New Model Salesperson:** *"That's not a problem. I'm curious, though, what would you like to ask them when you call?"*

This helps you find out whether they have a concern.
Or

> **New Model Salesperson:** *"Sure, that's not a problem. Just so I can send the right people to you, what specifically would you like to discuss with them?"*
> **Prospect:** *"Well, I want to find out from them . . ."*
> **New Model Salesperson:** *"That makes sense, when do you plan on calling them so I can let them know to see if they are available for you?"*
> **Prospect:** *"Well, I would probably just call them tomorrow afternoon if that works."*

New Model Salesperson: *"I can reach out to them to see if that works for them. Now, let's pretend for a moment that the clients you talk to say good things about how we were able to solve the same type of problems your company is having, where do you think we should go from there?"*

WARNING: If you simply agree to send a prospect reference without a commitment to know what the next step is after they talk to them, then you will most likely never hear from that prospect again.

How to Address the "Can You Send Me More Information?" Question

What about if, at the beginning of a call, the prospect asks you this dreaded question, *"Can you send me some information?"* Here's how you handle that one:

Prospect: *"Can you send some information to my email?"*
New Model Salesperson: *"That's not a problem. Just so I can put together the best information for you, what exactly are you looking for?"*
Prospect: *"Well, I'm looking to see how your XYZ product could . . ."*
New Model Salesperson: *"OK, and who/what do you use now for your* [insert service, product here]*?"*

Then you simply start going through the engagement stage with your first situation question; it's a very natural way to go from just sending some information to helping the prospect uncover their problems and start to engage with you. You're digging here and hitting pay dirt!

After you have taken them through the engagement stage, toward the end of the conversation, you will bring up the question they asked about sending them more information like this:

New Model Salesperson: *"OK, I can go ahead and send you more information about how we could solve those challenges you mentioned. Let's suppose you go through the information, and it fits into what you are looking for. What would you want the next step to be?"*

WARNING: Never, never, never send out information to a prospect without first finding out whether this is a serious person wanting to change their situation. Otherwise, you are just wasting valuable selling time.

How to Address the "I'm Too Busy Right Now" Response

Here's another overplayed one:

> **Prospect:** *"Can you call me back? I'm too busy right now."*
>
> **New Model Salesperson:** *"That's not a problem. What I can do if it helps you is give you my number and you'll have to call me back later today to see whether I would be available. Would that help? My number is 573-578-9872. What's your time frame on getting back to me today just to see whether I would be available for you?"*

Asking them what their time frame is just to see whether *you* would be available for *them* is a very powerful question that helps position you as a trusted authority in the market. It makes it appear that you are *busy with other clients*, that you are neither desperate nor needy. They will start to view you more as an expert *whose time is valuable*, rather than just another salesperson trying to sell them something.

> **Prospect:** *"I can get back to you sometime later in the week probably."*
>
> **New Model Salesperson:** ***"Well possibly, though it might be harder to randomly get a hold of me. What I can do, though***, *if you have your calendar handy, is I could pull out mine so you can* ***book a specific time*** *with me, that way you don't have to chase me down and vice versa. Would that help you?"*

This also positions you as a trusted authority whose time is valuable, rather than just another salesperson who they can blow off at any time. Now if they don't call you back right at that time, wait two minutes and then you call them, it's that easy!

Now that we've navigated through a few expected pitfalls, and once you've gotten to the point where you are *the* trusted expert and authority whom your prospect has trusted with their problems, you will then ask three committing or closing questions that will allow you to masterfully move your prospects forward with you in the buying process. Yup, you've made it to the commitment phase. Commitment-phobes need not apply. Brace yourselves, we're on our way!

Chapter 11

The Commitment Stage

Unless commitment is made, there are only promises and hopes; but no plans.
—Peter F. Drucker

Mazel tov, you've made it to the commitment stage. That's huge. And don't worry, there will be no *Runaway Bride* situations here. We're going all the way to closing that sale. But first, consider the six principles of asking for a commitment:

1. People are far more likely to change behavior if you ask for a commitment than if you don't.
2. Commitment questions need to be comfortable for you *and* the customer. If you're squirming, so is your prospect.
3. Great commitments start with pre-call planning. Be prepared for anything from pushback and interrogation to delays and downright ghosting.
4. Make commitment questions easy to ask.
5. Commitments are the natural, appropriate end to a conversation.
6. Asking for the seriousness of the commitment after someone says they are committing is perfectly acceptable and will increase sales if you do it well.

Look at these statements and questions. Do you know what all these phrases have in common?

> *"I'm just calling to see whether you would be interested in . . . ?"*
> *"Can I come by and show you what we can do for you?"*
> *"How about we schedule another call to move this forward?"*
> *"I can meet with you tomorrow at noon or Friday at three. Which time works for you?"*
> *"Do you still want to move this forward?"*
> *"When should I follow up with you?"*
> *"At the end of the call, we can see whether this is a good fit for you?"*
> *"At the end of the call, you can make an educated decision!"*

Yup, they're lame, and they are overused, but the answer we're looking for is that *they all trigger sales pressure and resistance.* There are certain words and language you may not even realize you're using that trigger pressure and resistance in your prospects. You must learn these words and phrases and avoid them like you dodge your chatty neighbor at the supermarket if you want to get to the top in your sales profession and one day move away from that neighbor.

You ready? Here's a good one—or, rather, a no good, very bad, horrible one. Wait for it:

> *"Just sign the contract here."*

Never, ever say this unless you want your prospects to run for the lifeboats as the band—and your sales pitch—plays on to an audience of none. Why? It will make most of your prospects feel that they are getting locked into something they might not want or may later regret. So what should you say instead to make the statement more neutral?

> *"Just authorize the agreement here."*

Yup, that's it. Simple and neutral. Of course, "authorize the agreement here" means exactly the same thing as "sign the contract," but it's *far* more neutral and so much less off-putting. Your customer is OK with *authorizing* an agreement to move forward with your solution.

The government does a crazy good job at this. Take a look at the IRS. It stands for Internal Revenue Service. If it were called *Internal Taxing Service*, which means the same thing, we would all be up in arms, but the term *revenue* is far more neutral and less threatening than the word *tax*, right?

If you adopt a more natural and neutral tonality with the words you use, it will allow for a more "trusting" connection to happen. Remember: human, not *humanoid* sales robot.

Say you're coming to the end of a conversation with a prospect, and then you try to "close" them on getting another appointment with you.

> *"Why don't we schedule another call soon to talk more about our solution for you?"*

But what would happen if you attempted to close them on having another appointment with you when they haven't even decided that they are ready to move forward with you yet in the first place? What if, no offense, they just don't want to have another appointment with you?

You would automatically trigger sales resistance from the prospect, right? They would push back and throw out objections, they would try to stall, or more than likely try to get rid of you, correct? As soon as there's pressure and resistance is triggered, that trust is kaput, ixnayed, gonzo. You're done.

So, if you want to book an appointment, use more neutral language that means the same thing, but it takes the sales pressure out of the questions.

Here are some excellent examples:

> *"Mrs. Prince, with your permission, we can set up another appointment to see whether what we are doing here would work for your situation. Would that be appropriate?"*
>
> *"Would it be appropriate for us to talk again on the phone to see whether we could help you?"*
>
> *"Would it make sense for us to talk again to see whether what we are doing will fit into what you're looking for?"*

"How do you want to proceed from here, Mr. Wayne?"
"Where do you think we should go from here?"
"What do you see as the next step here?"
"What would be the next step, or how would you like to proceed from here?"
"Would you be open to us having another conversation to see whether we could possibly help you?"

When you use neutral questions such as these with your potential customers, you diffuse any sales pressure. It's like a sales massage. It gives your prospect the message that you are there for them and that you genuinely want to see whether you can help them. Most salespeople only massage their own egos and needs. This separates you from them. You are now a trusted adviser to them, not an annoying reason why they need not only a massage, but a couple of aspirin too.

Traditional Closing Questions

By now, you are probably starting to understand that traditional sales techniques force salespeople to play a numbers game that just doesn't add up, completely going against human nature. These techniques are designed to "push" the prospect forward rather than get the prospect to pull you in. These techniques revolve around going through the numbers to try to make a sale.

Ask yourself this: Are you going in for the "kill" with your closing techniques? Are you following the ABCs of Closing? Here's a real Throwback Thursday, a Flashback Friday, a total rewind from a veteran sales guru: "You gotta close so you can make some cake." File this under Amusing Outdated Nostalgia along with your Blockbuster Video card because that's all it is.

Have you ever considered, in the post-trust era, with trust at an all-time low, that your potential customers can pick up when you're trying to "close" them? As aloof as they may seem, as addicted to their smartphones as they may be, they can still tell that they're being given the hard sell.

The old closing techniques do nothing more than put pressure on your potential clients. How do you feel when a salesperson is trying to close you? Do you feel the pressure yourself? Again, we ask you, is water wet?

If you, yourself, feel that pressure, don't you think your prospect is feeling it too? They feel like they are being "closed" and chased by you. It's annoying and it's futile because what do most people do when they feel chased? They run! Fast. They naturally want to retreat from that sales pressure—and, if that pressure is coming from you, they're running away from you like you're Freddy Krueger, Jason Voorhees, and Leatherface all in one. The horror!

What exactly do you do when you feel pressure from a salesperson? You do one of two things:

1. Get defensive, throw out objections, and reject what they are offering.
2. Withdraw from them because they have overwhelmed you; ghost them and don't return their calls, emails, or text messages.

Now, ask yourself: do your prospects ever do these two things to you when you try to close them? If you react this way to salespeople who try to "close you," how do you think potential customers are going to react to you when you keep using these same traditional closing techniques?

Now, do we mean that you should get on a call and not make sales? Um, is water dry? No! Your goal is to make a sale on *every* call, but you have to keep that to yourself because the moment they feel like they are being sold is the precise moment that they start to shut down.

But you're in luck. The New Model system teaches you how to avoid the push-pull dynamic that often develops between you and your potential customer, starting with one of the biggest things you must always avoid in closing: assuming the sale.

In the post-trust era, assumptive selling is not just dead at this point, it's mummified and in a museum. Any training that teaches you to always "assume" the sale and look for the close is just outdated training that was taught in Flintstonian times by gurus with pet dinosaurs who haven't been in sales for decades or, worse, by lazy newer sales trainers who just copied and pasted what the Bedrock gurus palling around with Fred, Wilma, Barney, and Betty taught in the past.

Your potential client completely feels it when you're trying to assume the sale, and what happens when they do? They start throwing out objections, right?

The question must be asked: if you're getting all these objections, who exactly is causing this? Turn on your selfie mode because, hello, *you* are, and it's because of the way you were taught to communicate.

Let's say that you've approached the end of your presentation and you automatically assume that your potential customer wants your product, so you start feeling out the contract and the following happens.

> **Average Salesperson:** *"Now, in whose name will the contract be?"*
> **Prospect:** *"Well, I guess my name."*
> **Average Salesperson:** *"OK, what's your phone number? Your address? Your bank details?"*

Short of asking their social security number, passwords, and blood type, the average salesperson pretty much just freaked out the prospect. At this point, what does the (polite) customer usually do nine out of ten times?

> **Prospect:** *"Wait, I never said that I'm ready for this purchase! Why don't you leave me some information, and I can get back to you after I've had a chance to think it over?"*

Cue objection handling mode because it's a matter of your survival now. This is something that never made sales sense. The very same traditional closing techniques that teach you how to assume the sale—which you now know triggers sales resistance—require you to learn objection handling techniques to try to overcome the objections that were caused by the way you were taught how to sell.

Wait, what? It's so convoluted, don't even go back and read that sentence. It's just a lot of work and a waste of everyone's time. Why not learn how to make sure you don't even get the objection in the first place?

And what about that whole always be closing thing? It's closed. Forever. Why are you still clinging to it like Linus and his blanket? Even Charlie Brown is laughing. This is undoubtedly one of the very first things you learn as a salesperson from the old sales gurus. The question is, does it really work anymore in the post-trust era? This is when you get to the end of your presentation and you ask your closing question:

The Option Close: *"Do you want the red one or the blue one?"*

The Invitational Close: *"Why don't you give it a try?"*

The Assumptive Close: *"OK, I'll go ahead and schedule this. Do you want to take delivery Tuesday afternoon or Wednesday morning?"*

The Choice Close: *"Are we going to do the contract in your name or your company's name?"*

The Demonstration Close: *"If I could show you the very best investment you could ever make, would you want to see that?"*

When you use the words *"If I could show you,"* to whom does the focus immediately go?

It, of course, goes to *you*, and now you've put yourself in a position to have to prove to your potential customer that your product/service is just right for them.

This is when most salespeople rely on statistics, facts, and features to back up their claims. But once again, whose opinion is this? It's coming from you, right?

Keep in mind that every other salesperson is also telling them the same thing, that they are the best and the potential customer should go with them. Can you see how your potential customers are used to having every salesperson try to sell them something by claiming that their product is the best? If eye-rolls could talk. It's no wonder that people have become desensitized to hearing these kinds of statements.

Since we live in the post-trust era, it's no mystery that trust is dead in the marketplace. What this means is, if you use traditional selling techniques, you need to prove yourself to a skeptical prospect who is trying to prove you wrong. Exhausting, isn't it? So what's the solution? We start with changing our *languaging* (a term coined by Jeremy to mean, literally, doing language).

Using the example from before, you could try saying something like, *"If there was an investment out there that could get you the returns you are looking for, would that be of possible interest to you?"*

By using this language, you're in a much more neutral position that doesn't create any resistance, and you no longer have to prove yourself to your potential customer. You can apply this phrase to any industry.

New Model Salespeople are *always* neutral, whereas Average Salespeople are always one-sided, focusing on themselves and their world instead of their potential client's world. While the old sales closing techniques may sound good in theory, so did synthesizers in '80s pop music. The reality is that, in today's world, your potential customers won't fall for this anymore. They've been hearing the same stuff for decades! Yawn and pass us the noise-canceling headphones.

Stop trying to manipulate. People want to know that they are respected. Today's customer doesn't want to be talked *at* and sold *to*; they want to be asked, heard, and understood. If you think that the way to close sales is by being aggressive and pushy, and you continue using traditional closing techniques, you'll keep losing sales and tens of thousands of dollars that should be in your bank account.

And here's a novel concept: selling could be much more profitable *and* a more fulfilling experience for you and, most importantly, for your customers by changing the way you close. In the New Model of Selling, the salesperson doesn't even use the term "closing." It has a negative stigma, and it can be dehumanizing toward your potential customer.

How would you feel if you overheard a salesperson who was selling you something talk about how they had just "closed" you? Oof. Sounds scammy—and scummy, no? For most people, this wouldn't feel good. The New Model Salesperson prefers to use the word "committing," never "closing." It's a *commitment* to take the next step and purchase your solution.

It's absolutely critical that you remember that "committing" or what traditional selling refers to as "closing" is only 5 percent of the New Model of Selling. Why? Because the sale was already made in your potential customer's mind during the engagement process as you asked skilled questions and used real listening skills.

In their mind, you have now become a trusted authority; therefore, the most logical next step is for them to purchase your solution from you. At this point in the sales process, the commitment to move forward is a very natural step after you have repeated to them what *they told you* they were looking for and how your solution can help them.

Committing Questions

Committing, the art of sales formerly known as "closing," is the last of the prospect's many logical conclusions in the sales conversation.

By now, you've

- Demonstrated your understanding of the potential customer's problems
- Found the correct solution to solve your potential customer's problems
- Put the proposed solution into effect

You're on fire! But don't reach for the extinguisher just yet.

Commitment can take one of two forms:

1. 1. A commitment to take a series of intermediate action steps that will lead to the sale
2. 2. A commitment to purchase your solution and do business with you and your company

You will come to a point where you will need to decide what move to make. You'll either ask for the commitment to purchase from you or you'll suggest *taking another step in the discovery process for them to move toward making a final decision.*

Encouraging a solid commitment requires four things:

1. Establishing a positive mindset and fully understanding what you need to accomplish to move prospects forward.
2. Planning and crafting the right questions, knowing the delivery of how to ask them, and nailing your delivery.
3. Stating your hypothesis and asking questions so prospects will see this as a logical next part of the discussion so they can solve their problems and get what they want.
4. Listening to their response. It may be no—at first. That's not a rejection; it's a continuing part of a process.

What do you think is key to moving the prospect forward in the process at this point? There's only one thing to do: ask for a commitment to do something! If your potential customer needs to take more steps forward to make a decision, then this is where you will selectively use the sales tools that are available to you.

You will make a statement and ask one of the following questions *if* you feel they need more steps before they will purchase your solution:

"With your permission, what I'd like to suggest as the next step is that we . . ."

Go on, continue your sentence with one of the following:

". . . review more about your business plan you discussed."
". . . schedule a demo to go over how we can solve the problems you mentioned."
". . . meet some other members of the company."
". . . look more closely at some of the problems you discussed."
". . . have another meeting to see whether we can help you."
". . . go over the proposal on how we could possibly help solve those issues and get you where you want to be."

And you'll complete your statement by asking

"Would that be appropriate?"
"Would you be open to that?"
"Would you feel comfortable with that?"
"Would that work for you?"

You want to make your potential customer feel that they are part of the process instead of feeling like you are trying to pull the wool over their eyes like 99 percent of salespeople do. Get your prospective customer involved in the process so that they feel that you are there to help them and not just to make a sale.

Imagine taking a cooking class in which you're all ready to roll up your sleeves and start chopping, channeling your inner Food Network star, and you discover you're just there to watch the teacher do it. How lame is that? It's also a guarantee that your next cooking class won't be there. Audience participation is no different when it comes to sales.

That being said, do realize that different people move at different speeds. Sometimes it can take many smaller steps before the final one in which they buy from you.

To keep them involved you can also ask: *"What would you like to see next?"* or *"What would you like . . . ?"* until you have covered everything that is of interest to them.

You can also ask questions to see whether you and your prospect are on the same page because there's nothing worse than talking to someone who already finished the book when you're still on chapter 2. These are called checking for agreement questions, and they should also be used during your presentation to hold the attention of your prospect. These questions include the following:

"Would this help you?"
"What do you see as the benefits of all this for you?"
"Does that make sense?"
"Do you feel comfortable with what we have covered so far?"
"Are we on the same page?"
"What are your thoughts on that?"
"How do you see that helping you the most though?"

You can also ask questions to see whether they have any concerns such as

"Would you be comfortable with this?"
"How does this feel so far?"
"How does this look to you?"
"Is there anything you would like to address with me at this point?"

If you feel the potential customer is ready for the next step to buy into your solution and do business with you, here come the *most important* committing questions you will ever learn. These are what separates the top 1 percent of salespeople from average salespeople, that, if used properly, can take you from where you are now, to earning the maximum commission possible. It is within your reach! Keep going.

When you know at the end of the sales process that it's time to commit them to taking the next step and purchasing your solution, you will ask: *"Do you feel like this could be the answer for you?"* Or another way to ask it would be, *"Do you feel like this could be what you're looking for?*

These questions are very neutral, yet very powerful. If you have done your job during the engagement stage of the sales conversation, 95 percent of the time your prospective customers will say, *"Yes, I do."* Boom, bingo! But you're not there yet! Then, you will follow up with this *probing* question: *"Why, exactly, do you feel it is though?"*

Once again, you're going to ask more than just a surface question. Why? Because not only do they tell *you* why they feel your solution is right for them but they're also telling *themselves!* They are telling themselves why your solution is the best. When people tell you why they want to work with you, don't you think it's more persuasive than you telling them that they should work with you?

Imagine your kids emerging like the Creature from the Black Lagoon from two weeks' worth of laundry pileup and mess, coming up to you saying, "Guess what? I think I should clean my room today." Yes, you'd pass out, but how much easier and nicer is it than you having to convince them that their rooms are hazardous to their health? Same goes for your prospects, though hopefully they don't resemble swamp monsters or messy teenagers.

After your potential prospects tell you they want to work with you, then you will ask, *"Do you feel like this is something you can do/use/have that will get you where you're wanting to go?"* This is powerful because, in their minds, they get to look at your solution as long term. It's the real deal that will get them where they want to go.

You will then ask them again to clarify by posing *this* question: *"Why do you feel like it is?"* This is another NEPQ probing question. Again, they tell you *and* themselves why your solution is right for them. Then you will make your way to asking a third commitment question, saying something like:

> *"Well, I don't have anything else to go over with you. It looks like we covered what you are looking for. Really the next step would be to make some type of arrangement for your* (whatever you're selling)—*you can do wire or card, and at that point we will . . ."*

Here you'll tell them the next steps after they purchase. This, to be followed by

> *"Would that be appropriate? How would you like to proceed from here?"*

Or you could use this as a committing question:

"Where should we go from here?"

Only use this once you have truly learned NEPQ New Model techniques. This is a *Cobra Kai* blackbelt NEPQ question that is so effective, but you will need to know how to react if they say something you didn't expect.

This is also a very powerful committing question to use at the end that shows them you respect them and their opinions. It's important to remember that they have already persuaded themselves during the engagement stage of the sales process.

So logically, when you ask this question, most of the time they will just answer with something like, *"What do I need to do to purchase?"* or they might have a few concerns or questions that you can address. *That's* what it takes to get the commitment.

Remember, the close isn't always the end of business and can be the catalyst for the continuation of the discussion. Closing is a process, and even the best sales process can be improved by building positive business relationships.

Chapter 12

Taking the Business Relationship to the Next Level

Business happens over years and years. Value is measured in the total upside of
a business relationship, not by how much you squeezed out in any one deal.
—Mark Cuban

S
ome say it's not what you know, but who you know that matters. We dis-
agree. You need to know both. Building productive business relationships
is crucial to your success. Networking is the lifeblood of sales. To be liked
is not enough in the sales biz. You need to be trusted, respected, and valued. Is
that so much to ask? Well, yes, because there's no app you can download to make
yourself magically valued. You've got to put in the work. You also want the respect
to be mutual, obviously. Asking the right questions helps propel you into the
territory you want to be in. When you establish this trust and respect, your sales
are likely to flourish.

Committing questions are the ammo you need to shoot your commissions to
stratospheric proportions. The power you have once you give up what you *thought*
was power by trying to assume the sale and to "close" your prospects is next level.
Being saved as "Trusted Adviser/Authority/Maven/Guru" in your customer's phone
as opposed to having your name, number, and email completely blocked is priceless.

What do you think would happen to your sales conversions if your prospects viewed you as the trusted authority, the expert in your entire market, as opposed to just another annoying, dreaded, relentless salesperson? Here are some examples of how next-level, New Model sales *advisers* would sound in various industries:

> If you sell coaching: *"Do you feel like this is something you can do to get you where you're wanting to go in your life? . . . Why though?"*
>
> If you sell financial services: *"Do you feel like this is something you can do to get you where you are wanting to go with your portfolio or your investments or getting a higher rate of return? . . . Why though?"*
>
> If you sell life insurance: *"Do you feel like this is something you could have to protect your family when something happens to you? . . . Why though?"*
>
> If you sell real estate: *"Do you feel like this is the home for you and your family? . . . Why though?"*
>
> If you sell knee implants to doctors or are in medical device sales: *"Do you feel like this could be the fit you are looking for to really get your patients what they want?"*

Don't close your New Model sales toolbox just yet. We have a few more tools to add to it.

The Calendar Commitment

This is where you ask for the commitment at a point in time. The prior agreements are in place and are carried along in the dialogue, and your prospect feels their momentum. They've bought into you, and they now look at you as a trusted authority, so therefore, agreeing to do business with you is just a logical conclusion.

Now is absolutely the right time to ask for the commitment to move forward.

> *"In order to do this for you, would it be appropriate for us to get out our calendars and schedule the next steps?"*

Notice the way the calendar statement is phrased with *"In order to do this for you."* This shows that you *want* to carry out the potential customer's wishes.

The truth is that there are no tricks, no fancy moves, no viral TikTok dances, no special techniques. Just remember to always be detached from your expectations of making a sale, and instead, focus on learning whether or not there is a sale to be made in the first place.

But hang on. Don't get too cocky here. You need to still be cautious that you are not rushing the prospect and pushing your solution. You want to avoid placing any sales pressure whatsoever on the potential customer, especially at this point, because, assuming you've been paying attention here, you are at the point where it would be very, very hard for the potential customer to say no to you.

Once you've gotten to this point, you *can* tell them what the next steps are, and you can ask for a "conditional decision" such as *"If you were to go ahead . . . ? Can I ask when you would . . . ?" "Is this something you're looking for now?"* or *"When do you want to . . . ?"* Just fill in how your solution solves their problems.

Then, you're going to suggest the next step for your prospect to take, and you'll inform them of the next step that *you* will take.

You have four ways to generate next steps:

1. Actions the potential customer offers to take
2. Actions the potential customer wants you to take
3. Actions you offer to take
4. Actions you want the potential customer to take

Depending on your situation, the next steps can vary, and in many cases, the next step is the first stage of implementation, and it requires a series of tasks from both the salesperson and the potential customer.

If concerns block the agreement, you'll need to commit to any next step that allows you to keep the dialogue going while you help your potential customers resolve their own concerns by asking skilled questions.

Here are some final tips to keep in mind during this critical stage:

- Avoid any sales pressure—there should be absolutely *zero* pressure here.
- Use mirroring and positive body language such as nodding your head in agreement.

- Keep checking in with your prospect to make sure any suggested next steps are appropriate.
- Know that any conditional decision can be treated as a decision.
- Don't use the word "contract." Use "agreement" instead.
- Find out about and address any more concerns now. Ask again whether there are any other concerns your prospect wants to bring up.

As long as you follow the New Model system correctly, you've just helped your customer move forward and it's nearly a done deal. You are now the go-to for this person. You will notice how they'll treat you and respect you. In a professional, pressure-free sales dialogue, each of you will share a perspective. The potential customer paints a picture of their needs, and with your listening skills, you'll be able to ask highly skilled questions that allow you to arrive at a final decision that is a win-win for both you and the customer.

Business Development

Now that you're ready to crush it out there, just one more thing. If you plan to be in sales until the next, next generation of Kardashians are born, you can't just get cozy with what you've got. You need to be constantly developing your business by doing five key things:

1. Maintain the customer base you already have.
2. Grow your opportunities within that base.
3. Leverage your current base for future business.
4. Create new customers.
5. And most importantly, train to retain.

As Brad Lea, the leading authority on web-based training and a good friend of Jeremy's always says, "Is training something you did, or is training something that you do?" If you want to be a sales superstar and make hundreds of thousands a year or more in commissions, it's something that you do daily. If you're a business owner and you want your sales teams to consistently hit quota *every* month and scale your company to a level that most would only dream about, then it's something your reps must do daily!

Think about the great sports starts like Tiger Woods, Michael Jordan, LeBron James, Tom Brady, and Patrick Mahomes. Did they do *some* training a long time ago and then just stop? Again, uh, is water dry? No! They train every day, always looking to improve their skill sets so they get better. They know if they don't, their competition will crush them. The same is true in selling. If you don't train, you never improve, you never make more money, and you end up losing sales you could be making.

As you've seen throughout this book, traditional sales techniques get outmoded, outdated, and expire. You must constantly evolve with the tips we've provided you with here and adapt to the times. Check in with yourself from time to time to ask, *"Where is my current business?" "Where are opportunities for new business?"* and *"Where do I need to stop spending my time?"*

And don't be shy—ever. Actively seek referrals from your satisfied customers. Some aren't always so forthcoming and, as they say, "If you don't ask, you don't get," so always ask when it's appropriate. There are weak referrals and strong ones; the strong ones are when the person doing the referring makes the intro phone call or email. Stronger than that are when the person not only makes the intro but arranges a meeting with all three of you. These are your *hashtag* referral goals.

Ready for some breaking, great news? If you're following the New Model, you'll eventually do less and less cold calling, *and* you'll have a higher percentage of referrals instead. That could depend on your industry, but a lot of times, salespeople trained in this method end up not doing any cold calling at all! And you know what's great about that? Referrals are *much* easier to sell to than a random stranger if you have the right questions in your arsenal, so pay attention.

There's a right way to get referrals, and here is the framework:

New Model Salesperson: *"I appreciate the opportunity to be able to help you. Can I ask you, in your mind, how do you feel I've been able to help you the most?"*

Why do we ask this? Because they're going to tell *themselves* how you have helped them, and when they do that, they *own* it. Self-owning is the best kind of owning.

New Model Salesperson: *"With that in mind, who do you know that might be struggling with* [here's where you plug in the problem you just solved for them]*?"*

An example might look like this. Let's say you sell merchant processing. *"With that in mind, who do you know that might be struggling with overpaying for merchant processing?"*

Once they've suggested a friend or business associate, the New Model Salesperson then asks for more information. Note the way this is asked, or more specifically, the tone.

New Model Salesperson: *"Can you please tell me a little bit more about this person and why you feel I could help them?"*

Why do you want them to tell you more? It goes back to finding out more about the person before you call. But remember, we also want the person to *own* this. That way, they're more likely to contact this person and build you up.

New Model Salesperson: *"Well, how do you think it would be best to approach them? Do you feel like you should communicate to them first that I will be calling?"*

Why would we want to ask this question? Because we want the person making the referral to reach out to them. It's more powerful that way. When they reach out to the contact and say something like, "I'm sending you somebody that I think might be able to help you," you're more likely to get a hold of them and convert that referral.

New Model Salesperson: *"What do you think you should say?"*

Now, why do you want to know what they're going to say to that person? First of all, you want to be able to prevent them from saying anything that could create resistance with that person—anything too technical, inaccurate, or downright weird. It's key that you set this up right. So offer a suggestion to help communicate the right thing with the right words.

> **New Model Salesperson**: *"Can I suggest something to you? What if you talked about some of the challenges you had and that he's having right now, and how we've been able to solve those, would that be more helpful to him?"*

In most cases, they're going to think this is a great idea.

> **New Model Salesperson**: *"So besides X, is there anyone else you feel I could help?"*

The use of the words "you feel I could help" is key. First, you've made it about them and how *they* feel, and second, people are more likely to give you referrals if you're in it to help people.

Now let's discuss how to call your referrals.

First, we're going to look at what most salespeople would say when calling a referral:

> **Average Salesperson**: *"Hey, Mary, I'm Michael Scott with XYZ Company. Amy asked me to give you a call and said that you'd be interested in my company's services. She said you're wanting to take your business to the next level. Do you have two minutes to talk right now about how my company can get you the results you're looking for?"*

Notice who this was focused on—it was centered entirely around the salesperson and her solution, not on the prospect. That was the first mistake. And then there's the second fail. You never want to *assume* that, just because you get a referral, they're automatically going to be interested. Let us go back to elementary school and repeat, if you assume, you make an . . . you get it, right? Do not assume anything!

I've seen salespeople fail at this because when they call, they're so enthusiastic, assuming that the referral is automatically going to be interested. So, from the get-go, you need to *let go* of the outcome of the sale and focus on whether or not you can help them and on whether there's a sale to be made in the first place.

Remember, the top 1 percent of all salespeople are problem finders and problem solvers; they're not product pushers. If you're a product pusher, you'll always be viewed that way, and they'll never take you seriously, and while you're busy assuming, they'll be doing a Google search for the best price elsewhere.

When this happens, assuming they're interested, most people will throw up some sales resistance.

Let's continue with the scenario from above:

> **Prospect:** *"Yeah, I guess this is a good time."*
>
> **Average Salesperson:** *"OK, great, I know you're going to be excited about what my company can offer you today. You see, here at XYZ Company, we've been in business for ten years, and we've helped over four thousand businesses have success. Now let me tell you a few things we can do to help you get where you want to go, and then you can make an informed decision at the end, about working with us."*

When you try using a closing technique right from the very beginning, and you tell them what you can do with a sales pitch, and then say they can then make an informed decision, what do you think that person feels? This automatically creates sales pressure. There's enough pressure in the world today. You do not want to pressurize your prospect unless you want them to run for the exits.

If you're still using this phrase *"and then you can make an informed decision,"* you've got to get rid of it. Burn it. Shred it. Destroy it. It simply *does not* work anymore. Why do salespeople keep using this technique?

Think about golf for a minute. If you're not very good, you might play one really good hole out of eighteen. The rest aren't so hot, but it keeps you motivated to keep trying, to keep coming back to play. As in sales, if you get one out of eighteen calls, you're playing the numbers game, and by saying the verboten "informed decision" (shudder), the prospect already feels sales pressure from you.

We must get rid of that old way of thinking. If you want to be in the top 10 percent, 5 percent, or 1 percent in your company or industry, you have to think completely differently from what you thought before—to get away from the school of thought that's giving you the results—or lack thereof, rather—you are experiencing now.

So, if you use word vomit like "informed decision," prospects are thinking, *This salesperson is trying to close me, what can I say or do to get rid of him?* But wait! It gets worse! They're probably not even listening to what you have to say. You're not involving them in the process, and you're not asking them any questions to find out what their needs or problems actually are, so why should they be listening to you instead of their growling stomachs?

Now, let's take a look at what a top salesperson would actually do—someone who understands the New Model of Selling—and brace yourselves for some drastic differences. You ready? Oh wait, one more thing.

Never assume that just because you've gotten a referral, they're automatically interested. Your first objective is to find out about the person and what problems they have, if any. Remember: don't assume anything, ever.

Here's what to say when calling referrals:

> **New Model Salesperson:** *"Hi, is this John? This is Jeremy. A mutual friend/ business associate of yours, Amy, suggested I call you, as I recently helped her with X that was causing them to Y, and she mentioned to me that you might be experiencing the same challenges with that. Is this an appropriate time to talk?"*

Notice that here, the salesperson is focused on solving problems. That's the absolute best way to call.

Now, what do you do if the referral wants to meet you? Before you start jumping for joy, reel it in first. Here's how to start the conversation:

> **New Model Salesperson:** *"Amy, it's nice to meet you and let's do this: just so I don't go over things you have already talked about with Jim, perhaps you can give me your thoughts on what you have discussed with him and then what you'd like to cover so that we could focus on you and what you might be looking for?"*

The mighty "might" is the neutral term here. At this point, most people are not looking for a solution, and in fact, most don't even know they've got a problem. But it's your job to be a problem finder, and with the New Model, those problems will surface. Voilà!

What's most important now is that you start putting this into practice. Once you do, you'll see massive results.

Put yourself out there. Don't get too complacent. Speak at an industry conference when you can, attend networking events, and join the chamber of commerce. Also be a visionary and sniff out business opportunities where you least expect them—the guy dressed like your favorite team's mascot next to you funneling beers could very well end up being your next, biggest customer. OK, so that's highly unlikely, but really, you never know. But ABL: Always Be Looking.

Also realize that there are those out there who will never, ever buy from us. No matter if you followed everything we've taught you here to a tee, there are just those people with whom we never connect. It happens. It's human nature. Sometimes you do have to walk away. Most of all, you have to know what you want to accomplish. Write down your goals, develop a plan, and go get 'em.

The End (but Really Just Your Beginning)
New World, New Model, Who Dis?

It took twelve years of trial and error, of carefully watching every prospect's
reaction to my words, and I found that certain words would trigger sales
resistance and objections, so I had to eliminate those words and phrases.
—Jeremy Miner

Great salespeople are crystal clear about their intent. Before they pick up a phone or
walk into an office, their intention is always to do what is in the best interest of the
customer. They focus on customers and not on themselves and their products.
—Jerry Acuff

I n an ideal world, the most significant role a salesperson plays is opening customers' minds rather than closing them. Stop acting like a seller and start
thinking like a buyer. Old-school sales techniques just don't work anymore.
"The world is changing. Soon there will only be the conquerors and the con-
quered. I'd rather be the former," said W'Kabi in *Black Panther*. You now have the
tools to be a conqueror of sales. Use them!

As you now know, the old model of selling is focused on presenting and closing, but behavioral science tells us that we are least persuasive when we tell and

199

push. People buy based on their emotions. That is why if you are only asking the "right questions," but you don't know when to ask them, or your tonality sounds like a robot, your prospect will feel like they are being interrogated.

Instead, learn how to deliver the questions so they sound natural. It's like a Hollywood actor or actress. Think about Jeremy's two personal faves, George Clooney or Scarlett Johansson, for a minute. Everything they say in movies is 100 percent scripted, but does it feel scripted? Not at all. It feels natural, it feels human, and that's why you love watching them. If they didn't deliver as well as they do, they'd be on the cutting room floor or straight to streaming. Sales has to be the same way; we have to memorize our questions, know the tonality required, and understand how to deliver the questions so it feels organic and natural in conversation, even though it's really a well-crafted, well-honed, skilled conversation. But not all conversations feel that way. Your conversation with a potential prospect may feel forced. Instead, you can be more persuasive when you allow others to persuade themselves!

The biggest problem in sales is always the one you don't know you have. Once you identify it, however, then it becomes your responsibility to solve. Now that you understand the New Model of Selling and where you're at now with current sales ability compared to where you could be, buckle up, because your life is about to take a SpaceX trip into the sales stratosphere.

Most of what we understand about selling is based on a foundation of assumptions that have crumbled. According to Payscale.com, the average salesperson using the old model of selling is only making about $49,047 per year as it works against human psychology.[11] Prospects tend to get defensive, withdraw, and avoid when they can sense the salesperson is focused on their agenda. Remember to leave your ego and agenda back on the shelf with those books on old-school sales techniques. Leave the small talk there too.

The New Model of Sales does not start out with small talk and does not force salespeople to always be enthusiastic. It does allow prospects to persuade themselves, and it builds trust. Your *New* Model of Selling spends the majority of time engaging a prospect. It focuses on transitioning "salespeople" into trusted authorities focused on helping prospects find what they are looking for, instead of selling them something. The New Model removes the sales pressure on the salesperson and their prospects.

Never forget the importance of focusing on your prospects' problems, what caused them, and whether they have a desire to change their situation. But pace yourselves. If you present your solution too early in the conversation, it can work against you as you will come across as too eager to pitch your solution. Prospects will pick up on this and think you are not listening and therefore wasting their time since it appears you only care about selling them something. If you let go of your need to make the sale and leave that 5 percent of the process till the end, you will gain control of the sale instead of losing it when you are presenting. You got this!

The difference between a salesperson at the top of their field and one who is just meh is that a top salesperson is a problem finder. Your services as a salesperson are far more valuable when your prospects are mistaken, confused, or clueless about their problems. When you can help them identify their problems by asking skilled questions, listening, and pulling out their emotions, then your engagement process becomes a way to guide your prospects to a logical solution for these problems.

Focusing on your prospects and what they want will also decrease the anxiety of all involved. It's like sales CBD oil. Apply liberally. But have patience too. You're not going to start making millions in your sales job in the next twelve months. Making bank like that takes commitment, hard work, and learning new, more advanced persuasion skills to get to that level.

The step from zero to one is always the hardest. But you've taken that step already by deciding that you're ready to upgrade your operating system, that you're ready to hit an unlimited income ceiling, and you're willing to do what it takes to get there.

Along the way, never forget to think like a buyer. And today's buyer, as you know, is a graduate of the Google University of Armchair Omniscience. In other words, they come equipped with what they think is expertise in *everything*. They know your middle name, what fraternity or sorority you were in during college, and what your first pet's name was (do not answer those sneaky Facebook questions, peeps).

In the United States today, a prospective Toyota Camry customer can arm themselves with all types of information before ever stepping onto a car lot. They can go on the internet and find other dealerships offering the same car providing a wider variety of choices, within a certain radius of their home.

They can tap into their social media network or visit websites to discover each dealer's reputation and see whether other previous customers were satisfied. That's the sales version of walking into a haunted house. You never know what horrors you may find on Yelp. Buyers should beware, but yet, many think that if it's on the internet, it must be true.

They can visit online forums to see what current Camry owners feel about the car. They can check *Kelley Blue Book*, *Edmunds*, or Autotrader.com to find out the price used Camrys are selling for. Once they find a car they like, they can take the auto's VIN and with a quick online search, find out whether it's been in any accidents or had major repairs done.

For the most part, they're protected from unethical sellers. But, if they get any dirty dealings or end up feeling screwed or shafted, they can do more than simply gripe to their best friend. They can tell a few thousand of their Facebook friends, Twitter followers, or the readers of their blog. Some of them will share their posts with their social media friends, completely undermining the seller's ability to sell. It's rough out there.

Today's consumer is wiser, more informed, more prepared, and less trustworthy of anything that comes out of your mouth to begin with. They're also armed with social media, adding extra pressure on salespeople to walk out with a sale and a five-star Yelp review. It's not easy but change never is. And neither is sales. But it can be a lot easier and a lot more fun when you're engaging with people instead of piling on the outdated sales spiel.

Never forget that to sell is to be of service, finding out what people want, and helping them get it. It's all about problem finding and problem solving. And never, ever forget that the holy grail of selling is credibility. You know more about your product than Google does, and if prospective customers see you as credible, trustworthy, and knowledgeable, they are more likely to act on your suggestions and advice and not the advice of the old-school salesperson who is still using dial-up access to CompuServe.

Always remember the five rules of buying:

1. You will sell significantly more if you think like a buyer than if you act like a seller.

2. The quality of your business is directly linked to the desire of your pro-spective customer to want to have a conversation with you.

3. The size of your business is directly linked to your ability to ask a customer questions that provoke thought.

4. High-pressure environments tend to create little exchange, which results in a lack of meaningful dialogue.

5. Low-pressure environments create greater exchange and customer receptivity.

Also remember that, with the New Model, engagement with your potential customer is 85 percent of the sale. That's huge, but it's hardly a hurdle if you remember the steps to successful engagement, like the answers on *Jeopardy!* (new host, who dis?). They come in the form of questions:

1. Connection Questions
2. Situation Questions
3. Problem Awareness Questions
4. Solution Awareness Questions
5. Consequence Questions
6. Qualifying Questions
7. Transition Questions
8. Commitment Questions

Remember that only 10 percent of the New Model is presenting. Almost like a dating app minus the awkward silence and realization that their picture was from thirty years ago, you're simply taking the answers they gave you and matching the correct features and benefits to them.

A successful mindset designed for sales greatness is the belief that to be great in front of the customer takes a commitment to excelling at *messaging*, having mastery of the knowledge and language necessary to be seen as an expert, and building your business with valuable relationships with those whom you are engaging in this way. You're dealing with human beings, not numbers. They like to feel important and heard. You're human; isn't that what you like too?

Nostalgia is fun. It brings back memories of good times, good music, food, smells, sounds, but not necessarily sales. When it comes to sales, you now know that nostalgia has no place there unless, of course, you're selling collections of oldies CDs, in which case, well, never mind. Not so ironically, Charles Darwin may have said it best when he said, "It is not the strongest or the most intelligent who will survive but those who can best manage change." You can not only manage it but you can also master it. Go on, now; go forth into New Model sales mastery. You got this!

Links and Resources:

To take next steps, join our free Facebook group at https://salesrevolution.group/ and download the NEPQ 101 Mini-Course for free.

Acknowledgments

Here's acknowledging you the salesperson, the entrepreneur, the CEO, the sales leader for daring to pick up this book and read it.

It is what separates you from unsuccessful people. Those who stay small, doubt a better way, and keep pushing the learning of advanced skills down the road. Sadly, these folk will ultimately be left behind.

It takes a unique and expansive type of person who is serious about their career and skillset, to realize that perhaps they don't know everything about sales. That just maybe there *is* more to learn to deepen their impact and earn more for their families and the companies they represent.

Truth is, it is really us salespeople who are the catalyst for prospects being able to change their situation and get the results they want in life, and in business.

If we do not learn how to communicate more effectively, in a way that works with human behavior in today's post-trust era, then in effect we consign our prospects to remain in their status quo. Their problems stay the same - and nothing ever changes for them. Certainly, the responsibility to spark change rests on our shoulders!

In light of this, we salute your readiness to grow and evolve. May God bless you in applying the methodology outlined in this book. As you transition from long-taught traditional techniques (old model sales methods) to those that align with today's sophisticated, info age buyer (the New Model of Selling), know that we are with you, supporting your progress, each step of the way.

About the Authors

Jerry Acuff

J erry is the CEO and founder of Delta Point in Scottsdale, Arizona and is a Graduate of the Virginia Military Institute.

Delta Point works with sales and marketing leaders to implement innovative ways to sell and market in today's crowded marketplace. Their client list includes 18 of the top 100 companies in the world.

Jerry spent his career in the pharmaceutical business and was Vice President and General Manager of Hoechst- Roussel Pharmaceuticals. In his twenty-year tenure, he received the award for Salesman of the Year twice, and District Manager of the Year three times.

Jerry has been featured on MSNBC, The ABC Radio Network and in Sales and Marketing Management Magazine, Entrepreneur magazine, The Wall Street Journal, The Street.com, Investor's Business Daily, Fast Company, Selling Power, Readers Digest and, Selling Power Live.

He has been to the White House to share his views on healthcare reform and twice was an Executive in Residence at The Amos Tuck School of Business at Dartmouth College. He has been an Executive in Residence at Northern Illinois University 14 times and is a guest lecturer at the University of Virginia Batten School of Leadership.

Jerry is currently rated as one of the top six sales experts in the world and was named one of the 50 Best Salespeople of all time on a list that includes Steve Jobs, Benjamin Franklin, and Warren Buffet.

Jerry is the author of four best-selling business books on building valuable business relationships and thinking like a customer. 11 Universities use his first book, *The Relationship Edge in Business* published by John Wiley and Sons, in their marketing curriculum.

You can find Jerry at jerryacuff.com and follow him on social media at: linkedin.com/in/jerryacuff - and - facebook.com/JerryAcuffFan/.

Jeremy Miner

"The single most effective way to sell anything to anyone in is to be a problem finder and a problem solver... NOT a product pusher."

For Jeremy Miner, the embodiment of this philosophy has made him one of the wealthiest sales professionals on the planet. During his 17 year sales career he was recognized in the direct selling industry as the #45th highest earning producer out of more than 100 million salespeople, selling anything worldwide - Jeremy's earnings as a commission-only salesperson were in the multiple 7-figures, *every* year.

He is the Founder and Chairman of 7th Level, a global sales training company. 7th Level ranked #1,232 fastest growing company in the USA in 2021; and #391 fastest growing company in the USA in 2022 by INC magazine's *INC 5000 Fastest Growing Companies* list. By industry, 7th Level is the #1 fastest growing sales training company in the USA.

Jeremy's particular brand of sales training pioneers the unique use of behavioral science and human psychology within the sales process, reflective of his deep studies in the subject from Utah Valley University. This scientific method of selling, created by Jeremy, has helped over 439,000 salespeople and counting in 158 different industries over the last three years to 3x, 5x and even 10x their sales results.

Jeremy is a contributor for INC magazine and has been featured in Forbes, USA Today, Entrepreneur magazine, the Wall Street Journal and a host of other publications on the topic of sales, persuasion and role of psychology and human behavior in the buying process.

You can find Jeremy at 7thlevelhq.com and follow him on social media at: Instagram: @jeremyleeminer | Facebook: Jeremy Miner - and - salesrevolution.pro | YouTube: Jeremy Miner | TikTok: @jeremy_miner | LinkedIn: linkedin.com/in/ jeremyleeminer | Podcast: Closers Are Losers.

Endnotes

1 Lee Rainie, Scott Keeter, and Andrew Perrin, "Trust and Distrust in America," Pew Research Center, July 22, 2019, https://www.pewresearch.org/politics/2019/07/22/the-state-of-personal-trust/.

2 Edelman, "2021 Edelman Trust Barometer," Edelman, 2021, https://www.edelman.com/trust/2021-trust-barometer.

3 John Gramlich, "Young Americans Are Less Trusting of Other People – and Key Institutions – than Their Elders," Pew Research Center, August 6, 2019, https://www.pewresearch.org/fact-tank/2019/08/06/young-americans-are-less-trusting-of-other-people-and-key-institutions-than-their-elders/.

4 Marc Beaujean, Jonathan Davidson, and Stacey Madge, "The 'Moment of Truth' in Customer Service," McKinsey, February 1, 2006, https://www.mckinsey.com/capabilities/people-and-organizational-performance/our-insights/the-moment-of-truth-in-customer-service; and Devon McGinnis, "Customer Service Statistics and Trends," The 360 Blog from Salesforce, May 2, 2019, https://www.salesforce.com/blog/customer-service-stats/.

5 Asking Increases Liking.," *Journal of Personality and Social Psychology* 113, no. 3 (September 2017): 430–52, https://doi.org/10.1037/pspi0000097.

6 Wanda Thibodeaux, "Why People Don't Make Phone Calls Anymore, According to Psychology," Inc.com, November 30, 2018, https://www.inc.com/wanda-thibodeaux/why-people-dont-make-phone-calls-anymore-according-to-psychology.html.

7   Aja Frost, "Only 3% of People Think Salespeople Possess This Crucial Character Trait," HubSpot, April 16, 2016, https://blog.hubspot.com/sales/salespeople-perception-problem.

8   George Loewenstein, "The Psychology of Curiosity: A Review and Reinterpretation.," *Psychological Bulletin* 116, no. 1 (1994): 75–98, https://doi.org/10.1037/0033-2909.116.1.75.

9   Gerald Acuff "Why Aren't Your Prospects Buying?" December 14, 2017, https://www.jerryacuff.com/arent-prospects-buying/

10   Linda Richardson, "Critical Communication Skills – Version 2020," September 22,2015, https://lindarichardson.com/critical-communication-skills-version-2020/

11   "Sales Representative Salary," Payscale, accessed October 12, 2022, https://www.payscale.com/research/US/Job=Sales_Representative/Salary.

A free ebook edition
is available with the
purchase of this book.

To claim your free ebook edition:

1. Visit MorganJamesBOGO.com
2. Sign your name CLEARLY in the space
3. Complete the form and submit a photo of the entire copyright page
4. You or your friend can download the ebook to your preferred device

A **FREE** ebook edition is available for you or a friend with the purchase of this print book.

CLEARLY SIGN YOUR NAME ABOVE

Instructions to claim your free ebook edition:
1. Visit MorganJamesBOGO.com
2. Sign your name CLEARLY in the space above
3. Complete the form and submit a photo of this entire page
4. You or your friend can download the ebook to your preferred device

Print & Digital Together Forever.

Snap a photo

Free ebook

Read anywhere

Printed in the USA
CPSIA information can be obtained
at www.ICGtesting.com
JSHW021910301023
51111JS00006B/60

9 781636 980119